MySQL 9 QuickStart Pro

Administrative strategies to upgrade, migrate and optimize databases with MySQL 9

Kylan Fentark

Published by: GitforGits

Publisher: Sonal Dhandre

www.gitforgits.com

support@gitforgits.com

Printed in India

First Printing: January 2025

ISBN: 978-81-984316-2-2

Cover Design by: Kitten Publishing

Prologue

MySQL 9 is a beast! It's got all these new features and improvements that make our database better than ever. To me, it's a game-changer for database tech. It's got some awesome performance, scalability, and security upgrades that can help any organization. With its advanced query optimization, improved replication, solid transaction controls, and super powerful automation features, MySQL 9 is setting the bar for modern database management.

I wrote "MySQL 9: QuickStart Pro" to share my passion and knowledge with database admins and developers. This book reflects my journey in getting the most out of MySQL 9. I worked through real-world problems and figured out practical techniques to install, configure, and manage MySQL environments on Linux systems, making even the most complex jobs manageable. I learned firsthand how upgrading old systems, moving data from other platforms, and tweaking performance could make a database super efficient and reliable for apps. In this book, I'll walk you through the whole process. You'll see how I dealt with tricky parts of replication and making sure everything was always available, turning problems into chances to come up with new ideas. I'll show you how to optimize queries with smart indexing, common table expressions, and window functions, making your data work faster and smarter for your business. I'll also share my strategies for managing transactions to ensure data consistency, even under heavy loads, and for securing your environment with strong authentication, role-based access control, and encryption.

I've also added modern techniques for automating database workflows, reducing manual intervention and streamlining routine tasks with shell scripts, scheduled events, and integration with third-party solutions like Google Spreadsheets and AWS.

My aim is to empower you with the skills and confidence needed to build a resilient, high-performing MySQL 9 environment that can evolve with your business demands.

Content

Preface

This book is for DBAs and devs who are eager to dive into the world of modern database operations with MySQL 9. With clear-cut instructions and step-by-step demonstrations, you'll be up and running in no time. You'll learn to install MySQL 9 on Linux, upgrade existing systems, and even migrate data from other platforms like PostgreSQL. Every chapter covers a key part of database administration, like deploying and scaling instances, setting up replication for high availability, and optimizing query performance through smart indexing, buffer tuning, and performance analysis using tools like MySQL Workbench.

It's got real-life scenarios to help you understand how to manage transactions, balance isolation levels, and resolve conflicts so your data stays accurate and reliable, even under heavy loads. It also shows you how to secure your MySQL environment through strong authentication, role-based access control, and encryption techniques. On top of that, you'll learn how to maintain your database through automated workflows, scheduled events, and integration with external tools like Google Spreadsheets and AWS S3. Overall, this book builds strong confidence and competency to deploy, manage, and optimize your MySQL environment for future heavy-data demanding applications.

In this book you will learn how to:

- Learn ins and outs of setting up MySQL 9 with step-by-step instructions.
- Prepare for MySQL 9 with ease by upgrading and migrating legacy databases.
- Set up high availability with multiple master-slave configurations, replication, and failover to make it resilient.
- Use efficient indexing, CTEs, window functions, and query profiling techniques to optimize query performance.
- Exact adjustments to isolation levels, savepoints, rollbacks, and commits for careful transaction management.
- Implement strong authentication, role-based access control, and use advanced encryption methods.
- Create partitioning, normalization, and efficient data integrity constraints schemas for scalability.
- Use shell scripts, scheduled events, and third-party integration to automate routine tasks.
- Perform ongoing system performance monitoring with MySQL Workbench and Performance Schema.
- Quickly fix issues with configuration and replication to keep database running smoothly.

GitforGits

Prerequisites

If you are familiar with the fundamentals of database administration and are prepared to learn how to use MySQL 9 to power your modern database operations, then this is the book for you.

Codes Usage

Are you in need of some helpful code examples to assist you in your programming and documentation? Look no further! Our book offers a wealth of supplemental material, including code examples and exercises.

Not only is this book here to aid you in getting your job done, but you have our permission to use the example code in your programs and documentation. However, please note that if you are reproducing a significant portion of the code, we do require you to contact us for permission.

But don't worry, using several chunks of code from this book in your program or answering a question by citing our book and quoting example code does not require permission. But if you do choose to give credit, an attribution typically includes the title, author, publisher, and ISBN. For example, " MySQL 9 QuickStart Pro by Kylan Fentark".

If you are unsure whether your intended use of the code examples falls under fair use or the permissions outlined above, please do not hesitate to reach out to us at support@gitforgits.com.

We are happy to assist and clarify any concerns.

Acknowledgement

I owe a tremendous debt of gratitude to GitforGits, for their unflagging enthusiasm and wise counsel throughout the entire process of writing this book. Their knowledge and careful editing helped make sure the piece was useful for people of all reading levels and comprehension skills. In addition, I'd like to thank everyone involved in the publishing process for their efforts in making this book a reality. Their efforts, from copyediting to advertising, made the project what it is today.

Finally, I'd like to express my gratitude to everyone who has shown me unconditional love and encouragement throughout my life. Their support was crucial to the completion of this book. I appreciate your help with this endeavour and your continued interest in my career.

CHAPTER 1: GETTING STARTED WITH MYSQL 9

Overview

Here we are, at the start of our book that will lead you to understand the architecture of MySQL 9 and discover its new features. Here you will learn about MySQL 9's features and see how its architecture impacts speed and scalability. Along with detailed explanations of the new features, you'll see practical examples of how each one contributes to the state-of-the-art approach to database management. By doing this preliminary research, you will be ready to work with advanced features right away and will have a solid groundwork for our project.

The next step is to install MySQL 9 on Ubuntu, which is done through an interactive, guided process that checks our environment configuration. The instructions will be laid out in a way that is easy to follow. We can practice critical configurations and set up a secure instance. We will be prepared to face the challenges ahead with practical confidence by configuring our MySQL 9 instance according to best practices that will support the development of our sample project.

Finally, the Retail Inventory project is introduced to you. It will be our learning platform for the entire book. The project outline will be reviewed by you. It details the steps to build an order management system using MySQL 9's core features. Each concept you learn is reinforced with hands-on experience thanks to the approach's design, which involves continually applying new skills to a live project.

Explore MySQL 9 Features

We will see for yourself just how reliable and scalable MySQL is. It's a solid open database, and it's got a customizable engine that supports high performance, real-time analysis, and complex transaction workloads. We will love how its modular architecture lets you integrate different storage engines and extend functionality through plug-ins. As you work with MySQL, the fact that it can handle big data volumes while keeping things accurate makes it a key part of our database toolkit.

Evolution of MySQL

MySQL 6 Onwards

The most popular version of MySQL right now is v6, and it's a big step in the evolution of the database engine. Even though MySQL 6 wasn't used a lot in production, you can see that a lot of its experimental features set the stage for the versions that came later. At the same time, developers and database pros were already checking out advanced replication, storage engines, and query optimization.

Transition through Intermediate Versions

As MySQL keeps on evolving, you move forward through time. After MySQL 6, you'll see that the middle releases make improvements bit by bit. We will see that these updates make replication, scalability, and security better. We will see that these versions make the performance and strength of the engine better and better over time, getting it ready for the challenges of modern data applications. We will see that developers get excited as they adopt these improvements, and you'll notice the seeds of innovation that grow into later releases.

Arrival of MySQL 8

We then see MySQL 8 emerge as a significant milestone in the evolution of the platform. MySQL 8 brings features like better JSON support, improved indexing and optimizer capabilities, and enhanced security features. We are impressed by the way MySQL 8 addresses the needs of modern web and enterprise applications, providing a solid foundation for high-performance, scalable solutions. We note that many of these features set the stage for the even more groundbreaking changes that you are about to explore in MySQL 9.

New Capabilities in MySQL 9

Enhanced Performance and Scalability

In MySQL 9, you are experiencing a leap in performance that builds on years of iterative improvement. We see that MySQL 9 is designed to efficiently handle higher transaction rates and complex queries with minimal latency. We are introduced to advanced query optimization techniques and a reimagined execution engine that allows for faster data retrieval and manipulation. As you interact with the system, you notice improvements in parallel query processing and dynamic resource allocation, which enable our applications to scale seamlessly even under heavy workloads.

Revolutionary Storage Engine Improvements

We are now diving into the new storage engine enhancements that MySQL 9 offers. We see that the integration of next-generation storage engines provides better performance and more efficient data management. The new architecture optimizes data read/write operations, reduces disk I/O, and ensures higher concurrency. We find that the redesigned buffering mechanisms and smarter caching strategies are key to achieving near real-time processing speeds. These improvements enable you to manage larger datasets with ease, while maintaining high levels of data integrity and consistency.

Advanced Security and Data Protection

In the realm of security, you are exploring robust enhancements that ensure our data remains safe. MySQL 9 introduces improved encryption protocols for both data at rest and in transit. We see that security features are now more deeply integrated into the core engine, offering granular control over user privileges and access management. As you work with the new version, you experience enhanced auditing capabilities that allow you to monitor database activities more effectively. These changes are designed to meet the evolving needs of regulatory compliance and data protection, ensuring that you are better prepared to handle security challenges in a dynamic environment.

Improved Replication and High Availability

We are also discovering significant advancements in replication technology with MySQL 9. The new replication mechanisms offer near real-time synchronization across nodes, enabling you to maintain high availability and ensure continuous data availability. We see that multi-source and group replication configurations are now easier to deploy and manage, providing a more robust framework for disaster recovery. As you configure these features, you experience smoother failover processes and improved data consistency, which are essential for mission-critical applications. These enhancements maintain an uninterrupted service experience even during peak demand periods.

New SQL Features and Analytical Functions

MySQL 9 is bringing a host of new SQL features that expand the analytical capabilities of the engine. We are engaging with enhanced support for Common Table Expressions (CTEs) and window functions, which simplify complex analytical queries. We find that these features allow you to write more expressive SQL queries that can perform sophisticated data analysis directly within the database. As you apply these new functions, you see improvements in query clarity and performance, enabling you to derive insights from our data with greater efficiency. This makes MySQL 9 a powerful tool for both transactional and analytical workloads.

Optimized Concurrency and Transaction Management

We are noticing that MySQL 9 has refined its transaction management system to support higher levels of concurrency. The engine now manages locks and isolation levels more efficiently, reducing contention during high-volume operations. We see that these improvements result in smoother and more reliable transaction processing, even when multiple operations are running simultaneously. As you interact with the system, you are able to execute complex transactions with confidence, knowing that the underlying engine is designed to maintain data integrity and consistency in demanding environments.

Enhanced Developer Experience

Finally, you are experiencing enhancements that improve the overall developer experience. MySQL 9 offers a more intuitive set of tools and interfaces that simplify database management and application integration. We see that the updated command-line utilities, along with improved documentation and community support, make it easier for you to adopt and adapt the new features. This user-friendly approach is designed to become productive quickly, enabling you to focus on developing innovative solutions rather than wrestling with complex configurations.

As you work through these features, you'll gradually become more confident in our ability to handle advanced database operations with MySQL 9, which will prepare you for the hands-on challenges and opportunities that await you on our project.

MySQL 9 Architecture

Now, we are going to take a closer look at how MySQL 9's engine architecture works. We will see how design improvements and enhancements at the engine level affect performance and scalability. We will take a peek at how MySQL 9's architecture supports its strong features and plays a key role in managing data for our sample retail inventory and order management system.

Core Engine

At the heart of the system, you encounter the query execution engine, which interprets SQL commands and translates them into actions on data stored in various formats. We see that the optimizer has received significant improvements, allowing it to better choose execution plans based on current statistics. The storage manager works in tandem with the query engine, orchestrating read and write operations with precision. We observe that internal buffers and caches are tuned to handle a high volume of simultaneous queries, ensuring that our application remains responsive even during heavy transactional loads.

Enhanced Query Execution

The latest version of MySQL, 9, makes query executions faster and more accurate. It has an improved optimizer that assesses multiple execution paths more accurately. We will see that this optimization minimizes the latency of complex queries, especially ones that join multiple tables or use nested subqueries. We will also be able to reorder operations dynamically, which is great for handling high-frequency data operations in our sample project. The enhancements in query caching and plan reuse also make the system faster, which is important in real-world scenarios.

Storage Engine Integration

The architecture supports a bunch of different storage engines, which are great for all sorts of use cases, like processing transactions and doing analysis. As you work on our project, you'll see that InnoDB is still the go-to engine, and it's got some pretty cool features like better concurrency control and crash recovery. We will also notice that the engine now handles data compression and indexing better, which means it uses less disk space and performs better when you're doing queries. We will also see that pluggable storage engines give you a lot of flexibility, letting you pick the best engine for the job, depending on the data type and how our workload looks.

Caching and Buffering Enhancements

The architecture has a better buffer pool that handles caching of data pages, indexes, and metadata. We will see that this buffer pool is more adaptive, adjusting its size and behavior based on workload characteristics. As you execute queries and transactions, you'll notice that the enhanced caching system reduces disk I/O, ensuring that frequently accessed data remains readily available in memory.We will experience the benefits of faster query execution and reduced latency, which are essential for a responsive order management system. We will really notice the difference during peak operations, when the improved buffering makes a tangible impact on performance.

Concurrency and Transaction Management

The engine's transaction subsystem is now more efficient at handling simultaneous operations. We will see that row-level locking and improved multi-version concurrency control (MVCC) reduce contention between parallel queries. As you run multiple transactions in our sample project, you'll see a decrease in wait times and deadlock occurrences. The architecture balances isolation and performance, allowing you to maintain data consistency without sacrificing throughput. We will also see that the engine can scale across multiple cores, which is great for handling high-volume workloads. This is especially helpful for our retail application.

Engine Optimizations for High Performance

When you check out the various optimizations that the MySQL 9 engine implements to boost overall performance, you'll see that the revamped query parser makes interpreting SQL statements a breeze, cutting down on overhead.We will notice that adaptive query execution lets the system respond to changing data distributions and workload patterns in real time.The improvements in memory management, like dynamic allocation of cache resources and optimized buffer flushing algorithms, make sure the engine keeps up a high throughput even under tough conditions. As you test these features, you see that the architecture effectively reduces latency and improves the efficiency of data retrieval and manipulation for supporting the operational demands of our sample project.

We can link these improvements to our sample retail, inventory management, and order system. The changes to how the system processes queries, integrates the storage engine, and manages caching all work together to make sure our application handles a lot of data operations easily. We will notice that faster query processing means faster order fulfillment, and better concurrency management supports transactions happening at the same time without messing up our data. The engine's modular design gives you a lot of flexibility, so you can tweak the system to fit our app's specific needs. As you build and test our project, you'll see that the database environment scales well, stays solid under pressure, and lays the groundwork for a high-performance system. During this process, you'll be working with MySQL 9's engine, turning raw data operations into a super-charged performance powerhouse. We will see that every upgrade, like adaptive caching and streamlined transaction controls, is essential for creating an architecture that supports both current and future requirements. As you keep developing our sample application, you'll be able to apply these insights, ensuring that each part of the engine works together to provide top-notch performance in real-world scenarios.

Install MySQL 9 on Ubuntu

We're getting our Ubuntu environment ready to host MySQL 9, and we will do it step-by-step to make sure everything goes smoothly. We will be working hands-on, typing in commands and checking the results as you go. The whole process is designed to make sure you install a solid, secure version of MySQL 9 that will be the foundation for our sample application.

Update Your System

Before you begin installing MySQL 9, first you must update our Ubuntu package lists to ensure that you have the latest available updates.

For this, open our terminal and run the following command:

```
sudo apt update
```

The package manager gets the latest repository lists, and you know this step is key to avoiding compatibility issues with outdated packages.

Install Prerequisites

Next, you install the required packages that MySQL 9 depends on. These might include software properties and other utilities that ensure a smooth installation.

To do this, enter the commans as below:

```
sudo apt install -y software-properties-common dirmngr apt-
transport-https ca-certificates
```

With this, you confirm that the necessary prerequisites are installed, and you are prepared to add the MySQL repository.

Add MySQL APT Repository

We now add the MySQL APT repository to our system. This repository provides access to MySQL 9 packages that are maintained by Oracle. We can do this by downloading the repository package using **wget** as below:

```
wget https://dev.mysql.com/get/mysql-apt-config_0.8.22-
1_all.deb
```

Next, you install the repository configuration package:

```
sudo dpkg -i mysql-apt-config_0.8.22-1_all.deb
```

When you're installing it, you'll see a configuration screen. Just select MySQL 9 as the version you want and confirm. We will see that these options are there to adjust the repository to get the packages you need.

Update Repository Information

Once the repository is added, you can update our package lists again to include the new MySQL APT repository information:

```
sudo apt update
```

here, you will see that the package manager now lists MySQL 9 packages, confirming that our system is ready for installation.

Install MySQL 9 Server

With the repository configured, you now install the MySQL 9 server package with the following command:

```
sudo apt install -y mysql-server
```

We might be asked for configuration options during the installation. Just follow the on-screen instructions, entering any required parameters. As the process continues, you'll see the progress of package extraction, configuration, and installation. We will watch the terminal as MySQL 9 and its related components are set up on our system.

Secure and Verify Installation

After installation, you secure our MySQL instance by running the security script. This script helps you set a root password, remove anonymous users, and disable remote root logins. We start the script by entering:

```
sudo mysql_secure_installation
```

We are prompted to configure security settings step by step. We choose to set a strong root password and confirm that you want to remove anonymous users and disallow remote root logins. We follow the prompts, ensuring that our instance is secured according to our security preferences.

Once you have installed and secured MySQL 9, you now verify that the service is running. For this, you check the status of the MySQL service by entering:

```
sudo systemctl status mysql
```

We see that the service is active and running. We know that this confirms a successful installation, and you are ready to move on to configuring our instance further if needed.

MySQL Login and Basic Configuration

To interact with our new MySQL 9 instance, you log in as the root user with the following command and provide the root password when prompted:

```
sudo mysql -u root -p
```

After logging in, you may want to make a few basic configuration adjustments to suit our environment. For example, you can check the current settings with:

```
SHOW VARIABLES LIKE 'max_connections';
```

By doing this, you see the current value and decide if you need to adjust it. While the default settings are generally sufficient, you are aware that fine-tuning will be part of our ongoing configuration as you develop our project.

Also, you can exit MySQL by typing:

```
EXIT;
```

Now one very important step which everybody skips is as you finish installing MySQL 9, you clean up any residual files that you no longer need by running:

```
rm mysql-apt-config_0.8.22-1_all.deb
```

After following all these steps, you can confidently confirm that our system is tidy and that you've got everything in place to support the further development of our application.

Configure MySQL 9 Instance

Initial Configuration

We start by familiarizing yourself with the main configuration file, typically found at **/etc/mysql/my.cnf** or included via **/etc/mysql/mysql.conf.d/**. We open the file using our preferred text editor:

```
sudo nano /etc/mysql/mysql.conf.d/mysqld.cnf
```

We see that the file contains various settings that govern the behavior of the MySQL server. In this case, you focus on parameters such as **max_connections**,

innodb_buffer_pool_size, and **query_cache_size** to ensure that the instance can handle high traffic and large datasets.

While the default settings are adequate for initial testing, you are customizing them to optimize performance and security for production use.

Adjusting Key Configuration Parameters

Setting Maximum Connections

We increase the number of allowed connections to accommodate multiple simultaneous users or applications. Find the **max_connections** parameter in the configuration file and adjust it to a higher value, such as 250 or 500, depending on our expected workload:

```
[mysqld]
max_connections = 250
```

We save the changes, knowing that this adjustment prevents connection bottlenecks during peak times.

Configuring InnoDB Buffer Pool

Since our sample application will handle significant data operations, you set an appropriate size for the InnoDB buffer pool. This pool caches data and indexes, reducing disk I/O and speeding up query execution.

We adjust the parameter to use about 60-70% of our available RAM if our server is dedicated to MySQL:

```
innodb_buffer_pool_size = 4G
```

We commit the change, understanding that this setting directly influences our instance's performance under load.

Tuning Query Cache Settings

Even though modern workloads often minimize query cache usage, you decide to configure it for scenarios with repetitive read queries.

We either disable it or fine-tune it based on our workload:

```
query_cache_size = 0
query_cache_type = 0
```

We disable query caching if you are expecting a highly transactional environment.

Enhancing Logging and Error Reporting

To facilitate troubleshooting and ensure smooth operations, you adjust logging parameters. We enable the general query log for initial testing and then disable it in production to save resources, while ensuring the error log is active:

```
general_log_file          = /var/log/mysql/mysql.log
general_log               = 0
log_error                 = /var/log/mysql/error.log
```

We confirm that error logging is enabled, so you can track any issues that occur during high-load operations.

Securing Remote Connections

And if our production environment needs remote connections, you'll want to make sure our bind-address is set up right. For a more secure setup, you keep the bind-address to **127.0.0.1** and use SSH tunnels for remote management, or you adjust it carefully:

```
bind-address = 127.0.0.1
```

We verify that only authorized hosts can connect to our instance, ensuring that the environment remains secure.

Applying Configuration Changes

After adjusting the configuration file, you restart the MySQL service to apply the changes:

```
sudo systemctl restart mysql
```

We can also observe the terminal for any errors during the restart process. A successful restart indicates that our configuration changes are syntactically correct and effectively implemented.

Verifying Configuration

Once the server restarts, you are ready to verify that the instance is correctly configured and running as expected.

Checking Service Status

We check the status of the MySQL service to ensure it is active and running:

```
sudo systemctl status mysql
```

We see output that indicates the service is active. This verification gives you confidence that the instance is prepared for production-level tasks.

Verifying Configuration Parameters

Next, you log into MySQL to verify that our configuration settings have taken effect. For this, you log in as the root user:

```
sudo mysql -u root -p
```

At the MySQL prompt, you run the following commands to check critical parameters:

```
SHOW VARIABLES LIKE 'max_connections';
SHOW VARIABLES LIKE 'innodb_buffer_pool_size';
SHOW VARIABLES LIKE 'query_cache_size';
```

We see that the returned values match our expectations. This direct verification assures you that the configuration file modifications are active and that our instance is optimized for the intended workload.

Running a Diagnostic Query

Now, to further ensure that the instance is ready for our sample application, you needc to run a simple query that simulates a typical workload. For example:

```
SELECT COUNT(*) FROM information_schema.tables;
```

Here, you observe the prompt response from MySQL, confirming that the server processes queries efficiently. We take note of the query execution time as a baseline for future performance tuning.

Monitoring System Performance

We can also use MySQL's built-in performance monitoring tools. For instance, you check the status variables that give insight into the current load:

```
SHOW GLOBAL STATUS LIKE 'Threads_connected';
SHOW GLOBAL STATUS LIKE 'Innodb_buffer_pool_read_requests';
```

We assess the performance data to ensure that the server is handling connections and data retrieval operations as intended. We keep these metrics in mind as you later integrate our retail inventory project, where performance becomes a critical factor.

With all the above tasks, you are now equipped with a finely tuned database instance that serves as a strong foundation for our project's ongoing development and future expansion.

Retail Inventory Project Overview

In this section, you are introduced to the GitforGits application, a hands-on system that manages book orders and inventory in a scalable manner. We are outlining a project structure that demonstrates the core functionalities of MySQL 9 while integrating advanced database concepts into a practical application. We are preparing to work on a system that handles book cataloging, order processing, inventory control, customer records, and supplier details—all while keeping the design flexible enough to accommodate future growth and additional features.

System Architecture and Core Modules

We design the system with a modular architecture that separates responsibilities across various components. The project starts with a clear distinction between transactional operations and analytical tasks. At its core, you build the following modules:

Book Catalog Module

We manage the details of books available at the depot. This module covers book titles, authors, categories, pricing, and current stock levels. We are setting up functions to add, update, or remove book records, ensuring that the system scales to handle diverse genres and multiple editions while maintaining a clean, organized catalog.

Order Processing Module

We handle the complete lifecycle of customer orders—from order placement to fulfillment. This module captures order creation, payment details, shipping statuses, and delivery confirmations. We design it to support multiple payment methods and shipping options, ensuring that it can evolve with changing business requirements. As you work with transactional controls, you are ensuring that every order is processed reliably with complete data integrity.

Inventory Control Module

We track inventory levels in real time across different storage locations. We set up tables and relationships that monitor stock movements, manage reorder levels, and record transactions for both incoming shipments and outgoing orders. We structure the module to support scalability with partitioning and effective indexing, ensuring that even as the volume of books increases, performance remains consistently high.

Customer and Supplier Management Module

We create a comprehensive database for customers and suppliers, capturing essential information such as contact details, order histories, and payment terms. We design this module to allow easy updates and detailed queries, supporting personalized customer experiences and efficient supplier communications. Maintaining relational integrity and dynamic query capabilities is central to this module.

Analytics and Reporting Module

We prepare the system for real-time analytics by designing a module that aggregates data across orders, inventory, and customer interactions. We set up views and stored procedures using advanced SQL features like Common Table Expressions (CTEs) and window functions, integral to MySQL 9. This module empowers you to generate insights about sales trends, inventory turnover, and order fulfillment efficiency, thereby supporting strategic decision-making.

Scalability and Integration Considerations

We build GitforGits Book Depot with scalability as a primary objective. The architecture is designed to handle a growing number of transactions and an expanding book catalog without sacrificing performance. Following are some key scalability considerations you integrate into our design:

Modular Data Structure

We design the database with clearly defined tables and relationships that allow you to add new modules seamlessly. As you expand the book catalog or introduce new features like customer loyalty programs, you rely on a normalized schema that minimizes redundancy and supports efficient queries.

Partitioning and Indexing

We structure the order and inventory tables with partitioning in mind, particularly as data volume increases. We set up indexes on frequently queried columns—such as book IDs, order dates, and customer identifiers—to ensure that query performance remains optimal. We experiment with different indexing strategies to balance performance and storage.

Replication and High Availability

As our project grows, you plan to implement replication configurations that distribute load across multiple servers. We prepare our design to integrate master-slave or group replication setups, ensuring that data stays synchronized and the system remains resilient under high traffic conditions. We also explore failover mechanisms that maintain system availability even during maintenance or peak loads.

Dynamic Resource Management

We design the system to scale dynamically by adjusting key configuration parameters, such as the InnoDB buffer pool size and connection limits. We use performance monitoring tools and system metrics to instruct these adjustments, ensuring that resource allocation scales in tandem with increased demand.

Integration with External Systems

We are preparing the system for seamless integration with external applications, such as e-commerce platforms, payment gateways, and shipping services. The modular design ensures that APIs or data exchange mechanisms can be added with minimal disruption. We incorporate data import/export utilities and scripting solutions that facilitate smooth integration, keeping the GitforGits Book Depot system flexible and adaptable.

As you build this project, you continuously apply MySQL 9 features like for instance, when designing the Book Catalog Module, you are using advanced SQL features like CTEs to simplify complex queries that aggregate sales data and inventory levels. In the Order Processing Module, you are applying transaction controls that ensure data integrity during simultaneous order submissions. We are also experimenting with performance tuning techniques, such as query optimization and index adjustments, as you simulate workload conditions typical of a busy book depot.

We are encouraged to populate the database with sample data that represents real-world scenarios—books, customers, orders, and suppliers. This sample data enables you to test query performance, verify data relationships, and monitor system behavior under realistic conditions. We also set up triggers and stored procedures that automate routine tasks, such as updating inventory levels when an order is confirmed or sending alerts when stock falls below a threshold. Throughout this process, you remain engaged with the system, frequently testing and verifying that each module functions as expected. We use diagnostic tools and performance metrics to fine-tune the system, ensuring that GitforGits Book Depot not only meets current needs but also scales effectively as our project evolves. Every concept you learn is directly applied to real components of the system, transforming theoretical knowledge into practical skills that you can leverage in professional settings.

Summary

To sum up, we looked at how MySQL 9 changed from earlier versions and found improvements that made it faster and more scalable. We learned how its improved query execution, better integration of storage engines, and better caching mechanisms helped process data faster and handle more transactions. We learned about the redesigned architecture that made these improvements possible, and we saw how changes to concurrency management and transaction control helped keep data correct when there were a lot of requests. We carefully planned each command to make sure that the final installation of MySQL 9 on Ubuntu was safe and effective. By fine-tuning important parameters like connection limits, buffer pool size, and logging options, you set up the instance and make it ready for production.

We also learned about how the GitforGits application, which was used as an example throughout the chapter, can be scaled up. We got to see how theoretical ideas can be used in the real world through this project's modules for cataloging books, processing orders, keeping track of inventory, and managing customers. Overall, we turned hard ideas into useful skills that gave people a solid base for running and expanding modern database systems.

CHAPTER 2: UPGRADE AND MODERNIZE ENVIRONMENT

Overview

The next step in upgrading and modernizing our environment is to install MySQL. In this chapter, you'll look at our current system and make sure the upgrade to MySQL 9 goes smoothly. When you look at our current setup, think of possible problems, and plan the migration process, you are following useful, step-by-step instructions. Each step tells you the right way to upgrade so that our data stays safe and there is as little downtime as possible. We are getting our environment ready for the next step by using interactive commands and steps that make the upgrade process easier and get our system ready for new features.

We are also dealing with old data by making sure it works with MySQL 9 and making any changes that are needed. We are actively taking part in processes that clean and format old data, making sure that all of it works well with the new version. Each task is made to keep things running smoothly and prevent data from changing. We are doing hands-on activities that feel more confident and skilled in handling old data during the upgrade.

In the last step, you tune and validate the system after the upgrade to make it run better. To make sure that our upgraded environment meets production standards, you are testing configurations, making changes to settings, and keeping an eye on metrics. By following these steps, you can create a modernized environment that is optimized, robust, and prepared for advanced MySQL 9 applications.

Assess and Execute Upgrade

Assess Current Environment

Before executing the upgrade, we will first check the version of MySQL running on our system. To understand this topic better, we will consider that we are currently using MySQL 5. So, let us open our terminal and run the following command to confirm MySQL 5:

```
mysql --version
```

We observe the output and verify that the installed version is indeed MySQL 5. We are now reviewing our existing configuration and data structure to ensure compatibility with MySQL 9. We take note of custom configurations, plugins, and extensions that might require adjustment during the upgrade process.

At this point, you are preparing a checklist of changes that may affect our Book Depot project once the upgrade is completed.

Backup Existing Data

We are now creating a complete backup of our MySQL 5 databases using the **mysqldump** utility.

For iths, we execute the following command to back up all our databases:

```
mysqldump --all-databases --user=root --password >
all_databases_backup.sql
```

Here, we confirm that the backup file is created and stored securely. This step is essential, as it provides a fallback in case any issues arise during the upgrade process. We also back up our MySQL configuration files, which you can locate in directories such as **/etc/mysql/** on Ubuntu.

Prepare Upgrade

With a complete backup in place, you are ready to proceed confidently with the upgrade. We are now updating our package lists and installing prerequisites that may be required for the upgrade.

So, now on our system, you execute:

```
sudo apt update
sudo apt install -y software-properties-common dirmngr apt-
transport-https ca-certificates
```

Next, you add the MySQL APT repository that provides access to MySQL 9 packages. We download the repository package using **wget**:

```
wget https://dev.mysql.com/get/mysql-apt-config_0.8.22-
1_all.deb
```

We then install the repository configuration package:

```
sudo dpkg -i mysql-apt-config_0.8.22-1_all.deb
```

With the repository now set to provide MySQL 9 packages, you update our package lists again:

```
sudo apt update
```

This step ensures our system is aware of the new MySQL 9 packages available for installation.

Execute Upgrade

We begin with installing the new version by running the following command to upgrade our MySQL server:

```
sudo apt install -y mysql-server
```

We monitor the terminal as the package manager downloads and installs MySQL 9 along with its dependencies. We notice that during the installation, you may be prompted to review configuration settings. We follow the prompts, selecting options that align with our production needs for our book depot project. The installation process replaces the old binaries and updates the system libraries to support the new version.

After the installation is complete, you restart the MySQL service to apply the changes:

```
sudo systemctl restart mysql
```

We verify that the service restarts without errors by checking its status:

```
sudo systemctl status mysql
```

The output confirms that MySQL 9 is running successfully, indicating that the upgrade process has completed as planned.

Verify Upgrade

We log into our newly upgraded MySQL 9 instance to ensure that the upgrade was successful. Using the command below, you log in as the root user:

```
sudo mysql -u root -p
```

At the MySQL prompt, you check the version to confirm the upgrade:

```
SELECT VERSION();
```

The result should display MySQL 9.x, confirming that you are now running the latest version. We then proceed to examine key configuration variables to ensure that they are optimized for production use. For example, you run:

```
SHOW VARIABLES LIKE 'max_connections';
SHOW VARIABLES LIKE 'innodb_buffer_pool_size';
```

We review the outputs to verify that the settings align with our expectations, as configured in the previous steps. If necessary, you plan to make further adjustments based on the specific needs of our project.

The upgrade process is all done and dusted, and we've got the green light to say that our MySQL 5 setup has been transformed into a solid MySQL 9 one. This upgraded environment is all set to handle the advanced features and performance boosts our app needs.

Handle Legacy Data

In the previous topic, you've successfully upgraded our server, but you know that older data structures, deprecated features, or non-standard configurations may not perform optimally under the new version. So here, we will learn to examine our legacy data, identify potential issues, and optimize it to fully leverage MySQL 9's enhanced capabilities.

Assess Data Compatibility

We begin by examining our legacy data for compatibility issues. First, you log into our MySQL 9 instance and connect to a database that contains legacy data. We run basic queries to see if the tables and data are accessible:

```
USE your_database;
SHOW TABLES;
SELECT * FROM legacy_table LIMIT 10;
```

As you execute these commands, you check for any errors or warnings that might indicate problems with data types, missing values, or deprecated functions. We pay special attention to features that were common in MySQL 5 but have been changed or removed in MySQL 9. For example, you review the usage of certain SQL modes, reserved keywords, or old storage engine parameters and document any issues that arise.

Identify Deprecated Features and Incompatibilities

Next, you identify any deprecated features that might affect our legacy data. We use the MySQL documentation and error logs to spot these issues. For example, you check if our SQL mode is too permissive or if you are relying on behaviors that have changed in MySQL 9.

For this, we run the following query to see the current SQL mode:

```
SHOW VARIABLES LIKE 'sql_mode';
```

We compare the output against the recommended SQL mode for MySQL 9. If you find deprecated modes or conflicting settings, you note these and prepare to adjust them. We also examine stored procedures, triggers, and functions that may rely on outdated syntax. As you review these objects, you consider updating the logic to use modern SQL constructs that are better supported in MySQL 9.

Verify Data Integrity and Structure

Once you have a clear picture of potential compatibility issues, you move on to verifying data integrity and structure. We use the **CHECK TABLE** command to assess whether any tables are corrupted or misaligned:

```
CHECK TABLE legacy_table;
```

This command provides a quick check of each table's status. We also run consistency checks on indexes and relationships by using the following command:

```
ANALYZE TABLE legacy_table;
```

As you run these commands, you carefully note any warnings or errors. We might find that some tables require repair or re-indexing. If you encounter such issues, you plan to run:

```
REPAIR TABLE legacy_table;
```

and then re-run **ANALYZE TABLE** to ensure that the data is now in proper condition.

Optimize Data Formats and Structures

After verifying data integrity, you focus on optimizing data formats and structures for MySQL 9. For instance, if our legacy schema uses outdated data types like **TEXT** for values that could be better served by **VARCHAR**, you prepare to alter these columns.

Here, we execute commands such as:

```
ALTER TABLE legacy_table MODIFY COLUMN column_name
VARCHAR(255);
```

This change not only modernizes the schema but may also improve query performance by reducing unnecessary overhead. We also review columns with numerical data, ensuring that they use the most appropriate types (e.g., **INT**, **BIGINT**, or **DECIMAL**) based on the range of values.

Migrate and Rebuild Indexes

Indexes that were built in MySQL 5 might not be optimized for MySQL 9's execution engine. So here, we are learning to rebuild these indexes to take full advantage of the new query optimizer. We start by dropping and then re-creating indexes on tables where performance lags.

For example:

```
ALTER TABLE legacy_table DROP INDEX old_index;
ALTER TABLE legacy_table ADD INDEX new_index (column_name);
```

We monitor the query performance before and after these changes by running sample queries and comparing execution times using the **EXPLAIN** command:

```
EXPLAIN SELECT * FROM legacy_table WHERE column_name =
'value';
```

This interactive process allows you to observe improvements and fine-tune indexing strategies. By rebuilding indexes, you ensure that our queries are executed with maximum efficiency under MySQL 9.

Update Stored Procedures, Triggers, and Functions

Legacy stored procedures, triggers, and functions may rely on syntax or behaviors that have been updated in MySQL 9. We log into the MySQL shell and review these objects using commands like:

```
SHOW PROCEDURE STATUS WHERE Db = 'your_database';
SHOW TRIGGERS FROM your_database;
```

We then examine the code for any deprecated functions or constructs. For instance, if you notice that a stored procedure uses an outdated loop or error handling mechanism, you update the logic to match MySQL 9's improved standards. Editing these objects might involve:

```
DELIMITER $$
CREATE PROCEDURE updated_procedure()
BEGIN
    -- new logic here
END $$
DELIMITER;
```

As you update these components, you test them thoroughly to ensure they behave as expected. This proactive approach prevents runtime errors and guarantees that all database operations will function seamlessly after the upgrade.

With all optimizations in place, you simulate real-world scenarios by running a series of test queries and transactions that reflect typical operations of our application. We use sample data and transactions to simulate book orders, inventory updates, and customer queries. This testing phase allows you to verify that the legacy data now operates correctly under MySQL 9's environment.

For example, you might run a complex join query that aggregates data from multiple tables:

```
SELECT b.title, o.order_date, c.name
FROM books b
```

```
JOIN orders o ON b.book_id = o.book_id
JOIN customers c ON o.customer_id = c.customer_id
WHERE o.order_date >= '2024-01-01';
```

We observe the execution plan and performance metrics to confirm that the optimized data is delivering the expected improvements in speed and reliability.

While you're working on this, please keep track of any changes you make to the legacy data and schema. We will put together a change log that'll outline any changes to data types, indexes, stored procedures, and other modifications for troubleshooting and future upgrades.

Post-Upgrade Tuning and Validation

With our legacy data optimized and the upgrade complete, you are now ready to adjust key settings and validate that our system operates efficiently under real-world conditions.

Adjust Key Parameters

We begin by reviewing the configuration parameters that directly affect performance. We log into our MySQL shell and execute commands to check current values for critical variables.

For instance, you run:

```
SHOW VARIABLES LIKE 'max_connections';
SHOW VARIABLES LIKE 'innodb_buffer_pool_size';
```

We assess whether the values meet the demands of our application. If you expect high user traffic or large data operations, you might increase **max_connections** to allow more concurrent sessions. Similarly, you adjust the **innodb_buffer_pool_size** to allocate sufficient memory for caching data, ensuring that frequently accessed information remains in memory rather than requiring disk reads. We modify these settings by editing the MySQL configuration file (usually located in **/etc/mysql/mysql.conf.d/mysqld.cnf**) and then restart the service:

```
sudo systemctl restart mysql
```

We take note of any changes and verify that they persist by re-running the variable check commands.

Optimize Query Execution

Next, we focus on query performance. Using the **EXPLAIN** command, you analyze how MySQL

9 executes our queries. For example, you run:

```
EXPLAIN SELECT * FROM books WHERE title LIKE '%Data%';
```

We review the execution plan to understand how indexes are used and whether any full table scans occur. Based on these observations, you refine our indexes and, if necessary, adjust query structures. We might also adjust parameters such as **join_buffer_size** or **sort_buffer_size** to further optimize performance for complex queries.

Monitor Performance Metrics

To validate that our tuning adjustments have the desired impact, you set up monitoring for key performance metrics. We use MySQL's performance schema and system variables to monitor metrics like query latency, buffer pool hit ratios, and connection utilization.

For example, you may execute:

```
SHOW GLOBAL STATUS LIKE 'Innodb_buffer_pool_read%';
SHOW GLOBAL STATUS LIKE 'Threads_connected';
```

These commands provide insight into how well our system is handling data retrieval and managing concurrent connections. We integrate this information with external monitoring tools to keep a real-time view of performance under load. We then simulate workload conditions by running batch queries and measuring their execution times. This validation step confirms that our configuration changes effectively enhance performance and that our MySQL 9 instance can handle the demands of our application.

Test Data Integrity and Application Workloads

Now that performance tuning is in place, you can now validate data integrity and overall system stability. For this, we can execute a series of test transactions and queries such as we can run transactions that simulate order placements and inventory updates as below:

```
START TRANSACTION;
INSERT INTO orders (customer_id, order_date, total_amount)
VALUES (101, NOW(), 49.99);
UPDATE inventory SET stock = stock - 1 WHERE book_id = 205;
COMMIT;
```

In this, we carefully monitor the results to ensure that transactions complete successfully and that no data corruption occurs. We also test error handling by simulating failures and checking that rollback operations work as expected. Through these tests, you confirm that our tuned environment maintains data integrity while processing complex, concurrent transactions.

Fine-Tune Resource Allocation

The performance of MySQL 9 depends on how effectively it manages system resources such as CPU and memory. So here, we adjust configuration parameters like **innodb_log_file_size** and **innodb_flush_method** to ensure optimal disk I/O performance.

For example, you might set:

```
innodb_log_file_size = 512M
innodb_flush_method = O_DIRECT
```

These changes help reduce the overhead associated with disk writes, especially in high-transaction environments. We test the impact of these adjustments by comparing query response times and transaction throughput before and after the changes.

Summary

In short, by switching from an older MySQL 5 setup to the newest MySQL 9, we have learned a lot about how to improve and update our MySQL environment. First, we looked at the current system, made sure we knew what version it was, and made full backups of our data to keep it safe. We did an organized upgrade, adding the right repository and installing new packages while keeping a close eye on each step to make sure everything went smoothly. We made sure the upgrade was successful by looking at the version numbers and key configuration parameters to make sure the new environment was up and running and set up correctly.

We knew that old data might not work perfectly with MySQL 9, so we ran test queries and looked at the error logs to see if the data was compatible. We changed data types, rebuilt indexes, and updated stored procedures and triggers to get rid of deprecated features and make the most of old data structures. Lastly, we fine-tuned the improved system by changing important settings like buffer sizes and connection limits. We also ran stress tests and query analysis to make sure the system worked well. We learned important skills in data migration, optimization, and performance tuning, which helped us make our GitforGits's database environment strong and up-to-date.

CHAPTER 3: MIGRATE FROM OTHER SYSTEMS

Overview

This chapter focuses on adding an external PostgreSQL database to our MySQL 9 environment so that you can move data from other systems into our application. We will learn how to make a detailed migration plan that takes into account the main differences between MySQL and PostgreSQL and makes sure that all data types and relationships are properly mapped and kept.

After that, you will change the data types, make changes to the constraints, and keep the referential integrity of the PostgreSQL schema. We will be able to see firsthand how to solve problems with compatibility and bring unique PostgreSQL features to MySQL by doing this hands-on exercise. We will learn how to change our schema so that it works best in the new environment and get useful information about the subtleties of differences in SQL syntax.

Lastly, to fine-tune our MySQL setup, you will match up data types and indexes. Because you optimised the converted schema and rebuilt the indexes, our database will work well and be ready for the needs of a dynamic, production-ready system. Every step in this chapter is meant to give you the skills you need to successfully move data between databases and give you more confidence in our ability to handle future data integrations.

Prepare Migration

Let us think or consider that our application needs to integrate an external PostgreSQL database to enrich our book depot system with additional data. In this scenario, you face the challenge of merging two different worlds: the robust, feature-rich PostgreSQL environment and our modern MySQL 9 system. So here, we begin by sitting down with our team, reviewing both systems side by side, and planning how to bridge the differences while ensuring a smooth data transition.

Understand Source and Target Environments

Now, put yourself in the shoes of someone examining the current PostgreSQL database. We will open up our go-to database management tool and start checking out the schema. We will spot tables with custom data types, unique functions, and special extensions that PostgreSQL offers — features that show just how flexible it is. We will take a close look at how it handles JSON data, arrays, and other advanced constructs.We will document each weird and wonderful aspect, pointing out the potential challenges these might pose when mapping them into MySQL 9's structure. This helps you understand the main differences between the two systems. It gets you ready for a successful migration.

Next, we check out our current MySQL 9 setup, which powers the application. We think about how MySQL 9's enhanced performance features, optimized storage engines, and modern SQL capabilities are already making a difference in our project. As you review the schema, you notice that while MySQL 9 and PostgreSQL share similar relational principles, their implementations are quite different. We're learning about how MySQL 9 manages data, like how it supports Common

Table Expressions (CTEs) and its unique indexing approaches. This helps us understand what adjustments we will need to make to make PostgreSQL data work well with the MySQL 9 environment.

Defining Migration Objectives and Scope

We sit with the stakeholders—database administrators, developers, and business analysts—and discuss the goals of the migration. The conversation centers on ensuring that the integration maintains data integrity, minimizes downtime, and preserves the functionality essential for managing book orders and inventory. We articulate that the migration should support both current operational needs and future scalability. With everyone on the same page, you outline clear objectives: maintain data accuracy, map PostgreSQL-specific features to their MySQL equivalents, and ensure that the new system can handle a high volume of transactions seamlessly.

Together, you set tangible goals for the migration process. These include:

- Preserving the integrity and accuracy of data throughout the transition.
- Achieving a seamless migration with minimal disruption to the GitforGits Book Depot operations.
- Ensuring that every feature in PostgreSQL has a corresponding implementation in MySQL 9.
- Preparing a detailed mapping for data types, stored procedures, and triggers that differ between the systems.
- Establishing a baseline for performance that can be validated once the migration is complete.

These goals provide a roadmap that reassures the business side that the migration will be handled with precision and care.

Developing a Detailed Migration Plan

Schema Mapping and Data Type Conversion

Imagine yourself drafting a comprehensive document that maps every element of the PostgreSQL schema to its MySQL 9 counterpart. We note that PostgreSQL's **`SERIAL`** data type, used for auto-incrementing fields, will correspond to MySQL's **`AUTO_INCREMENT`** integer. We also compare the handling of JSON data, where PostgreSQL's functions and operators might need reworking to fit MySQL 9's JSON data type and functions. As you write down each mapping rule, you also mark sections that require custom scripts for transformation. This document becomes our bible during the migration process, as every discrepancy is accounted for and that no data is left behind.

Identifying Dependencies/External Integrations

Now here, we explore the external systems that depend on the PostgreSQL database. We recognize that our GitforGits isn't an isolated system—it interacts with third-party applications, external APIs, and custom scripts. We make a list of all dependencies, noting how each one connects to PostgreSQL. We plan for updates to connection strings, drivers, and API calls, ensuring that these external touchpoints are ready for the switch to MySQL 9.

We've worked on projects before where older data was a real pain. So, we will be doing a deep data audit of the PostgreSQL setup to find any problems with data that's not in sync, has null values, or is using outmoded formats. We might run some queries to find duplicate entries and messed up dates, and then write up scripts to fix the data. This proactive approach helps you spot issues and design solutions that'll let you fully optimize the data once it's transitioned to the new system.

Establishing a Migration Timeline

Phased Migration Approach

Since a big-bang approach could lead to downtime and unexpected problems, you decide on a phased migration strategy.We will outline a plan where you first migrate a subset of non-critical data as a pilot project.This phase lets you test the mapping rules, data transformation scripts, and integration points in a controlled environment.By comparing performance and functionality between PostgreSQL and MySQL 9 during this phase, you can fine-tune our approach before migrating the full dataset. This slow rollout is a good way to avoid risk and make our team and stakeholders feel more confident.

Rollback and Contingency Planning

Every plan needs a safety net, so we make sure to document a strong rollback strategy in case something goes wrong during the migration. We also specify clear steps to get the PostgreSQL environment back if critical issues pop up, making sure that no data gets lost and operations keep running smoothly. On top of that, we schedule regular backups and define recovery points that will serve as checkpoints throughout the migration process. This level of preparedness is crucial because it shows that we've thought of every potential problem and have a plan to deal with it.

Testing and Validation Strategy

Pre-Migration Testing

Before initiating any data transfer, you design a comprehensive testing strategy. We create test cases that mirror real-world scenarios, including typical queries, transactions, and batch operations from the GitforGits. These tests provide a baseline for performance and functionality in the existing PostgreSQL environment, and they will serve as a benchmark for evaluating the MySQL

9 setup after migration.

Post-Migration Validation

We plan a detailed validation process to be carried out after the migration is complete. This involves running the same set of tests on the MySQL 9 instance, comparing the results to ensure that data integrity is maintained and that performance meets the established benchmarks. We schedule user acceptance testing sessions where stakeholders verify that the system behaves as expected and that all business-critical functionalities are intact.

This whole meticulous planning ensures that when you eventually perform the conversion, you can do so with confidence, knowing that all potential challenges have been anticipated and addressed.

Convert PostgreSQL into MySQL

Imagine that you are now ready to convert a sample PostgreSQL database into MySQL 9 format for our GitforGits application. So here, you work with a PostgreSQL database that manages book information, customer orders, supplier details, and inventory records. We are tasked with transforming the PostgreSQL schema into a MySQL-compatible format while preserving all the critical data relationships. This whole process involves exporting the PostgreSQL schema, mapping data types, adjusting constraints, and importing the schema into MySQL 9.

In our sample PostgreSQL database, you have several key tables:

- **books:** Stores information about books, including a unique identifier, title, author, category, and price.
- **customers:** Contains customer data such as customer_id, name, contact details, and address.
- **orders:** Records customer orders with fields like order_id, customer_id, order_date, and total_amount.
- **suppliers:** Maintains supplier information for book restocking.
- **inventory:** Tracks stock levels with references to book_id and quantity.

We notice that PostgreSQL uses features such as the **`SERIAL`** data type for auto-incrementing primary keys, and it supports specific data types like **`TEXT`**, **`VARCHAR`**, and **`TIMESTAMP WITHOUT TIME ZONE`**. So our goal will be to translate these constructs into MySQL 9 equivalents while keeping the referential integrity intact.

Export PostgreSQL Schema

We begin by exporting the PostgreSQL schema using the **`pg_dump`** utility. Open our terminal and run the following command to export only the schema (without data) into a file named **bookdepot_schema.sql**:

```
pg_dump --schema-only --no-owner --file=bookdepot_schema.sql -
-dbname=your_postgres_db
```

We review the generated SQL file and see definitions for tables, constraints, indexes, and triggers. This file is our starting point for transforming the schema.

Transform Data Types and Syntax

Next, you open the **bookdepot_schema.sql** file in our favorite text editor and begin with mapping PostgreSQL data types to our MySQL equivalents. For example:

- Replace **SERIAL** with **INT AUTO_INCREMENT**.
- Change **TEXT** to **LONGTEXT** or **VARCHAR(65535)** depending on usage.
- Convert **TIMESTAMP WITHOUT TIME ZONE** to **TIMESTAMP**.

We work through each table definition. For instance, the PostgreSQL definition for the **books** table might look like this:

```
CREATE TABLE books (
    book_id SERIAL PRIMARY KEY,
    title TEXT NOT NULL,
    author TEXT,
    category VARCHAR(100),
    price NUMERIC(10,2)
);
```

We manually adjust this for MySQL by replacing data types and syntax:

```
CREATE TABLE books (
    book_id INT AUTO_INCREMENT PRIMARY KEY,
    title VARCHAR(255) NOT NULL,
    author VARCHAR(255),
    category VARCHAR(100),
    price DECIMAL(10,2)
```

```
) ENGINE=InnoDB;
```

We ensure that the new definitions are compliant with MySQL 9 standards. For the **customers** table, you might perform similar modifications, ensuring that unique constraints and default values are correctly defined.

Adjust Constraints and Relationships

We then move on to transforming constraints and relationships. PostgreSQL supports the **REFERENCES** keyword for foreign keys similarly to MySQL, but you need to verify the syntax.

In our PostgreSQL schema, the **orders** table might have a foreign key defined as follows:

```
CREATE TABLE orders (
    order_id SERIAL PRIMARY KEY,
    customer_id INT REFERENCES customers(customer_id),
    order_date TIMESTAMP WITHOUT TIME ZONE DEFAULT now(),
    total_amount NUMERIC(10,2)
);
```

We modify it to match MySQL syntax:

```
CREATE TABLE orders (
    order_id INT AUTO_INCREMENT PRIMARY KEY,
    customer_id INT,
    order_date TIMESTAMP DEFAULT CURRENT_TIMESTAMP,
    total_amount DECIMAL(10,2),
    FOREIGN KEY (customer_id) REFERENCES
customers(customer_id)
) ENGINE=InnoDB;
```

We repeat this process for every table that involves foreign keys, indexes, or unique constraints, ensuring that all relationships remain intact. We double-check that any composite keys or multi-column indexes are properly defined.

Create Consolidated MySQL Schema File

Once you have manually transformed all the table definitions, constraints, and indexes, you compile the updated SQL statements into a new file, perhaps named **bookdepot_mysql_schema.sql** as this file now contains the MySQL 9 compatible schema for our GitforGits application.

We review this consolidated schema file thoroughly. As you read through it, you verify that each table has the correct engine (preferably InnoDB for transaction support), that data types are appropriate, and that all relationships between tables are clearly defined. At this stage, you might also add any MySQL-specific enhancements, such as setting default character sets (e.g., **DEFAULT CHARSET=utf8mb4**) to ensure broad compatibility.

Import Schema into MySQL 9

With our MySQL-compatible schema file ready, you are now ready to import it into our MySQL 9 instance by running the following command:

```
mysql -u root -p < bookdepot_mysql_schema.sql
```

We enter our root password when prompted, and the schema is executed in our MySQL environment. We then log into MySQL to verify that all tables have been created successfully:

```
mysql -u root -p
SHOW TABLES;
```

We see that tables such as **books**, **customers**, **orders**, **suppliers**, and **inventory** appear as expected. This confirms that the conversion process has correctly transformed the PostgreSQL schema into a functional MySQL 9 schema.

Verify Data Relationships and Integrity

After importing the schema, you proceed to validate that the data relationships are intact. Although you haven't migrated data yet, you simulate some relationships by inserting test data into the tables.

For example, you might insert a sample record into the **customers** table:

```
INSERT INTO customers (customer_id, name, contact_details,
address) VALUES (1, 'Alice Smith', 'alice@gitforgits.com',
'123 Book St');
```

Then, you insert a corresponding record in the **orders** table:

```
INSERT INTO orders (customer_id, order_date, total_amount)
VALUES (1, NOW(), 59.99);
```

We run a join query to ensure that the foreign key relationship works as intended:

```
SELECT o.order_id, c.name, o.total_amount
FROM orders o
JOIN customers c ON o.customer_id = c.customer_id;
```

The successful execution of this query reassures you that the relationships between the tables have been correctly preserved in the conversion.

During the process, you may encounter minor discrepancies or errors due to subtle differences between PostgreSQL and MySQL syntax. For example, if a default value for a date column does not work as expected, you revisit the schema file and adjust it. We might also need to adjust the size of **VARCHAR** columns or modify the precision of numeric fields based on sample data performance. We systematically test each table and relationship, documenting any changes for future reference.

We also review the MySQL error logs in case of any issues during the import process:

```
sudo tail -n 50 /var/log/mysql/error.log
```

By monitoring these logs, you ensure that no critical errors went unnoticed and that every part of the schema is functioning as intended.

Reconcile Data Types and Indexes

In this section, you are focusing on fine-tuning our MySQL 9 database by reconciling data types and indexes. After converting the PostgreSQL schema, you now ensure that every data type and index is optimized for performance in our GitforGits application. We follow a practical, step-by-step approach that adjusts the converted schema, enhancing performance and ensuring that the structure is tailored to the operational characteristics of MySQL 9.

Identifying and Adjusting Incompatible Data Types

We start by reviewing the data types that were directly converted from PostgreSQL. Even though you mapped most data types correctly, you notice that some definitions might not be optimal in MySQL. For example, PostgreSQL often uses **TEXT** for variable-length strings, but in MySQL, a **VARCHAR** with an appropriate length can perform much better in indexed columns. We examine tables such as the **books** table and notice that columns like **title** and **author** should ideally be defined as **VARCHAR(255)** rather than **LONGTEXT** if they are frequently used in search queries or joins.

For this, we execute a query to inspect the table structure:

```
DESCRIBE books;
```

We then look for columns with data types that might slow down queries, such as unnecessarily large **TEXT** fields. In such cases, you alter the table to adjust the data type:

```
ALTER TABLE books MODIFY COLUMN title VARCHAR(255) NOT NULL;
ALTER TABLE books MODIFY COLUMN author VARCHAR(255);
```

After this, we apply similar modifications to other tables, ensuring that numeric data types, such as **NUMERIC** in PostgreSQL, are properly converted to **DECIMAL** or **FLOAT** as needed. These adjustments not only reduce storage overhead but also improve query performance, particularly when columns are indexed.

Rebuilding and Optimizing Indexes

Indexes are super important for query performance, and moving over to MySQL 9 could mean indexes that aren't fully optimized. So, first we are going to take a look at the indexes we already have on our tables:

```
SHOW INDEX FROM books;
```

This command lets you observe the current index structure on the **books** table. We compare these indexes with our query patterns. If you find that some indexes are redundant or that composite indexes can be merged for efficiency, you note these improvements.

For instance, if the **orders** table has separate indexes on **customer_id** and **order_date**, and you often run queries filtering by both columns together, you decide to create a composite index. We remove the redundant individual indexes and then create a new one:

```
ALTER TABLE orders DROP INDEX customer_id_index;
ALTER TABLE orders DROP INDEX order_date_index;
ALTER TABLE orders ADD INDEX idx_customer_order (customer_id,
order_date);
```

We also check for indexes on text columns, where a prefix index might be more efficient. If you have an index on a large **VARCHAR** column, you can specify a prefix length to reduce index size:

```
ALTER TABLE customers DROP INDEX name_index;
ALTER TABLE customers ADD INDEX idx_name (name(50));
```

These changes help cut down on the size and efficiency of our indexes, which means faster query response times. We also make sure that foreign key indexes are set up right to keep relational integrity without sacrificing performance.

Testing and Validating Adjustments

After reconciling the data types and rebuilding indexes, you need to test our changes to validate that performance has improved. We run a series of benchmark queries on the modified tables. For example, you use the **EXPLAIN** command to analyze the query plan:

```
EXPLAIN SELECT * FROM books WHERE title LIKE '%Data%';
```

We review the execution plan, ensuring that the indexes you created are being utilized effectively. If you observe any full table scans where indexes should be used, you note the discrepancies and adjust the schema further.

Automating Reconciliation and Future Proofing

As you refine our database, you also try to consider automating parts of the reconciliation process to save time during future migrations or schema changes. So here, we develop scripts that can regularly check for discrepancies between the desired schema and the current implementation. These scripts might use queries to compare expected data types and index configurations with those currently defined:

```
SELECT COLUMN_NAME, DATA_TYPE
FROM INFORMATION_SCHEMA.COLUMNS
WHERE TABLE_SCHEMA = 'bookdepot_db' AND TABLE_NAME = 'books';
```

The above automated checks can generate reports that flag any deviations from the optimized schema.

Throughout the process, you keep detailed notes of every change made and the performance impact observed. This documentation becomes a valuable resource for troubleshooting and future optimization. By reconciling data types and indexes, you ensure that the converted schema not only preserves data relationships but is also optimized for the unique performance characteristics of MySQL 9.

Summary

Moving from PostgreSQL to MySQL 9 went smoothly, and we learned a lot about how to work around the differences between the two systems. First, we looked at the PostgreSQL database, writing down its unique features and data types, and then we compared them to what MySQL 9 can do now. We were able to see possible problems and make a clear plan for how to convert the schema thanks to this critical analysis.

As we moved forward, we carefully exported the PostgreSQL schema and carefully changed it so that it would work with MySQL, making sure that all relationships and dependencies were kept. Throughout this exercise, we refined the schema by addressing issues such as the conversion of SERIAL to AUTO_INCREMENT and adjusting textual data types to more efficient VARCHAR fields. We additionally reconstructed indexes to improve query performance in the new environment, aligning them with MySQL's query optimizer. The changes we made led to a strong, high-performing schema that could support our application. This was confirmed by thorough testing and validation.

In the end, we wrote down every step we took and what happened. This helped us understand the difficulties of moving data between databases and gave us the skills we will need to manage future migrations and improvements in a real-world setting.

Chapter 4: Deploy and Scale MySQL Instances

Overview

This chapter teaches you how to set up and grow MySQL 9 instances to meet the needs of modern database programs, with our GitforGits application in mind. First, you will set up a single-node instance on Ubuntu. This is where you will set up important parameters, make sure our installation is safe, and make sure everything works properly. This basic step will give you the confidence to add more complex settings, making sure that our MySQL environment is strong and ready for use in production.

Next, you will explore how to manage multiple MySQL instances on a single machine, allowing you to isolate workloads and test different configurations. We will then dive into clustered deployments using MySQL Group Replication, where you will establish a multi-node cluster to achieve high availability and load balancing. In parallel, you will learn how to configure non-clustered setups with performance-oriented optimizations, focusing on fine-tuning resource allocation such as memory, CPU, and disk I/O. By doing these hands-on activities, you will learn how to create a database infrastructure that is scalable, efficient, and reliable.

Setup a Single-Node Instance

Until now, we are pretty well hands-on with the MySQL installation, upgrading, and schema migration. Now, we can proceed to configure a single-node instance that will serve as the backbone for our GitforGits application. But before you begin configuring our standalone instance, you confirm that the correct version is running, so you can proceed to configure the instance.

Configuring MySQL Instance

Locate Configuration Files

MySQL's primary configuration file is typically located at **/etc/mysql/mysql.conf.d/mysqld.cnf**. We open this file first:

```
sudo nano /etc/mysql/mysql.conf.d/mysqld.cnf
```

In this file, you find various settings that control how MySQL operates. We review these settings to understand their impact on performance and reliability. This configuration file will be our central point for optimizing the server for production use.

Adjust Basic Parameters

We first focus on essential parameters that ensure the instance is robust and can handle the workload of our GitforGits application.

First, we increase the number of allowed connections to accommodate multiple users and applications:

```
[mysqld]
max_connections = 250
```

You allocate a significant portion of memory to the InnoDB buffer pool, which caches data and indexes:

```
innodb_buffer_pool_size = 4G
```

We ensure that our instance uses the UTF-8-character set to support a wide range of text:

```
character-set-server = utf8mb4
collation-server = utf8mb4_unicode_ci
```

We also enable logging to help with troubleshooting and performance monitoring:

```
log_error = /var/log/mysql/error.log
general_log = 0
slow_query_log = 1
slow_query_log_file = /var/log/mysql/mysql-slow.log
```

We save these changes and exit the editor. These adjustments lay the groundwork for a stable, production-ready environment.

Restarting and Verifying Instance

After updating the configuration file, you need to restart the MySQL service to apply the changes:

```
sudo systemctl restart mysql
```

We check the status of the service to ensure that it restarted without errors:

```
sudo systemctl status mysql
```

A successful restart confirms that our changes have taken effect and that the MySQL instance is running as expected.

Testing and Initial Use

Logging into MySQL

To interact with our new instance, you log in using the MySQL client:

```
sudo mysql -u root -p
```

We verify that you can access the database without any issues and check that our configuration parameters are as expected:

```
SHOW VARIABLES LIKE 'max_connections';
SHOW VARIABLES LIKE 'innodb_buffer_pool_size';
```

Running Sample Query

We run a simple query to ensure that the instance responds quickly and correctly:

```
SELECT NOW();
```

The prompt and correct output of the current timestamp confirm that our MySQL instance is operational.

Configuring Backups and Maintenance

Here, we plan to set up automated backups using a cron job and the **mysqldump** utility. For example, you might create a script that runs daily to back up our databases:

```
#!/bin/bash
DATE=$(date +%F)
mysqldump --all-databases --user=root --
password='your_password' > /backup/mysql_backup_$DATE.sql
```

We save this script (e.g., **/usr/local/bin/mysql_backup.sh**), make it executable:

```
sudo chmod +x /usr/local/bin/mysql_backup.sh
```

Then, you add a cron job to execute the script every night:

```
sudo crontab -e
```

Add the following line:

```
0 2 * * * /usr/local/bin/mysql_backup.sh
```

At this stage, you have configured a single-node MySQL 9 instance and have adjusted core parameters to support high performance, set up regular backups, and ensured that the server is well-monitored.

Manage Multiple Instances

Before starting, you consider the reasons for managing multiple instances. We might want to isolate specific workloads, maintain separate configurations for testing, or achieve resource optimization. In our application, you decide that having a dedicated instance for intensive analytics, separate from our primary transactional system, could enhance performance and simplify troubleshooting. We plan to create each instance with its own configuration file, data directory, and listening port such that resource allocation, log management, and performance tuning can be managed independently.

Creating Separate Data Directory

The first step is to create a new data directory for the additional instance. We use the following commands to create a dedicated directory, ensuring that permissions are set correctly so that MySQL can access it:

```
sudo mkdir -p /var/lib/mysql_instance2
sudo chown mysql:mysql /var/lib/mysql_instance2
```

This new directory will house the databases for our additional instance, keeping its data isolated from the primary instance.

Setting up Custom Configuration File

Next, you create a custom configuration file for the second instance. We copy the existing configuration file and modify it as needed:

```
sudo cp /etc/mysql/mysql.conf.d/mysqld.cnf
/etc/mysql/mysql.conf.d/mysqld_instance2.cnf
```

Open the new file with our preferred text editor:

```
sudo nano /etc/mysql/mysql.conf.d/mysqld_instance2.cnf
```

Within this file, you make several critical changes, such as,

We change the default port (3306) to a different one, for example, 3307:

```
[mysqld]
```

```
port = 3307
```

We update the data directory path to point to the new directory:

```
datadir = /var/lib/mysql_instance2
```

We can specify a unique socket file to avoid conflicts:

```
socket = /var/run/mysqld/mysqld_instance2.sock
```

We also change the locations of error logs, slow query logs, and other files to keep them separate:

```
log_error = /var/log/mysql/mysql_instance2_error.log
slow_query_log_file = /var/log/mysql/mysql_instance2_slow.log
```

We save and close the file. All these modifications ensure that the second instance runs on its own port, with independent data and log management.

Initializing New Data Directory

With the custom configuration in place, you now initialize the new data directory for the second instance. Use the following command to set up the system tables:

```
sudo mysqld --initialize --user=mysql --
datadir=/var/lib/mysql_instance2 --defaults-
file=/etc/mysql/mysql.conf.d/mysqld_instance2.cnf
```

This command creates the necessary system tables and prepares the instance for first-time use. We carefully review the output to capture any temporary passwords or messages that may be required during the initial login.

Starting Second Instance

Once initialization is complete, you start the second instance using the custom configuration file. We can do this by specifying the configuration file when launching the MySQL daemon:

```
sudo mysqld_safe --defaults-
file=/etc/mysql/mysql.conf.d/mysqld_instance2.cnf &
```

Alternatively, if you are using systemd, you may create a new service unit file for the additional instance. For now, running it with **`mysqld_safe`** in the background confirms that the process starts successfully. We then check that the instance is running by looking for the unique socket file and verifying the port:

```
sudo netstat -tlnp | grep 3307
```

This command shows that the second instance is listening on port 3307. We can also check its status by connecting to it using the MySQL client:

```
mysql -u root -p --
socket=/var/run/mysqld/mysqld_instance2.sock
```

We log in and run a few simple queries, such as **`SELECT NOW();`**, to confirm that the instance responds as expected.

Managing and Isolating Multiple Instances

With both the primary and the second instance running, you now have the flexibility to manage workloads separately. We can adjust configuration parameters individually to meet the needs of each instance. For example, you might allocate a larger buffer pool for the primary instance if it handles critical transactions, while the secondary instance, dedicated to analytical queries, might have a different tuning strategy.

We also consider the benefits of isolating error logs and performance metrics. By having distinct log files, you can quickly diagnose issues that affect one instance without interfering with the other. Furthermore, this separation allows you to schedule maintenance and backups independently. For example, the secondary instance could have less frequent backups if it primarily handles read-heavy analytical tasks.

Configuring Systemd for Persistent Management

For a more permanent solution, you might opt to create a dedicated systemd service for our second instance. To do this, you create a new service file:

```
sudo nano /etc/systemd/system/mysql-instance2.service
```

In this file, you include the following content:

```
[Unit]

Description=MySQL 9 Instance 2

After=network.target

[Service]

User=mysql

Group=mysql
```

```
ExecStart=/usr/sbin/mysqld --defaults-
file=/etc/mysql/mysql.conf.d/mysqld_instance2.cnf
Restart=on-failure
LimitNOFILE=5000
[Install]
WantedBy=multi-user.target
```

We save and close the file, then reload the systemd daemon:

```
sudo systemctl daemon-reload
```

We enable and start the new service:

```
sudo systemctl enable mysql-instance2
sudo systemctl start mysql-instance2
```

We verify the service status:

```
sudo systemctl status mysql-instance2
```

This setup automates the management of our second instance, ensuring that it is consistently available.

Monitoring and Troubleshooting

As you manage multiple instances, you keep an eye on performance metrics and logs for each instance independently. We use monitoring tools to track CPU usage, memory allocation, and query performance. Checking logs frequently, such as the error log at **/var/log/mysql/mysql_instance2_error.log**, helps you detect and resolve issues early.

We also implement routine checks using system commands:

```
sudo systemctl status mysql-instance2
```

And by logging into each instance with the respective socket, you can run diagnostic queries to monitor internal status variables:

```
SHOW GLOBAL STATUS LIKE 'Threads_connected';
```

By isolating performance data for each instance, you ensure that any issues are quickly identified and resolved without affecting the other instance.

So, to get you up to speed, we've put together a step-by-step walkthrough to setting things up on a Ubuntu machine for managing multiple MySQL instances. First thing, we made a special data directory and set up a custom configuration file, then we got things going with an extra instance on a different port, and we even got systemd set up so that you have ongoing management. All of this gets you familiar with the ropes, so you can handle workload distribution, try different setups, and keep things running smoothly in such production-ready setting.

Implement Clustered Deployments

Before we begin, we ensure that you have at least three Ubuntu servers (or virtual machines) available. Each server must have MySQL 9 installed, and they must be connected over a reliable network. We also need to configure firewalls and network settings to allow communication on the ports used by MySQL Group Replication (typically 3306 for standard MySQL connections and additional ports for replication communication). In our planning phase, you decide on a three-node cluster to balance the load and provide redundancy, which is essential for a production environment.

Configuring Each Node

Update and Prepare Nodes

On each server, you start by ensuring that all packages are updated and that MySQL 9 is installed. We run:

```
sudo apt update && sudo apt upgrade -y
mysql --version
```

This check confirms that each node is running MySQL 9. We also ensure that each node has a unique server ID. We open the MySQL configuration file on each node and set a unique **`server_id`**:

```
[mysqld]
server_id = 1   # For node 1, use 2 for node 2, and 3 for node
3
```

Adjust Group Replication Settings

On each node, we add the necessary configuration settings for Group Replication. In the same configuration file, include settings such as:

```
[mysqld]
# Basic replication settings
log_bin = mysql-bin
binlog_format = ROW
gtid_mode = ON
enforce_gtid_consistency = ON
# Group Replication specific settings
transaction_write_set_extraction = XXHASH64
loose-group_replication_bootstrap_group = OFF
loose-group_replication_start_on_boot = ON
loose-group_replication_local_address = "NODE_IP:33061"
loose-group_replication_group_seeds =
"NODE1_IP:33061,NODE2_IP:33061,NODE3_IP:33061"
loose-group_replication_group_name = "book_depot_cluster"
```

We replace **NODE_IP** with the actual IP addresses of each server. These settings enable binary logging, enforce GTID consistency, and configure group replication to use a dedicated port (33061 in this example).

Create a Replication User

We need to create a dedicated replication user on each node. We log into MySQL on each server and run:

```
CREATE USER 'repl'@'%' IDENTIFIED BY 'secure_password';
GRANT REPLICATION SLAVE ON *.* TO 'repl'@'%';
FLUSH PRIVILEGES;
```

This user will be used by Group Replication for inter-node communication.

Bootstrapping Cluster

Starting Group Replication on First Node

On the first node, you perform the bootstrap process. We log into the MySQL shell and execute:

```
SET GLOBAL group_replication_bootstrap_group=ON;
```

```
START GROUP_REPLICATION;
SET GLOBAL group_replication_bootstrap_group=OFF;
```

This command starts the cluster with the first node as the initial member. We verify that Group Replication is active by checking the status:

```
SELECT * FROM performance_schema.replication_group_members;
```

We should see the first node listed as part of the group.

Adding Remaining Nodes

On the second and third nodes, you simply start Group Replication without bootstrapping:

```
START GROUP_REPLICATION;
```

We then log into each node and verify their status using:

```
SELECT * FROM performance_schema.replication_group_members;
```

As each node joins the cluster, you observe that the list of group members grows, confirming that all nodes are successfully connected and synchronized.

Verifying Cluster Functionality

Testing Data Consistency

With the cluster established, you now test data consistency across nodes. We insert a sample record into a database on the first node:

```
USE bookdepot;
CREATE TABLE test_cluster (id INT AUTO_INCREMENT PRIMARY KEY,
message VARCHAR(255));
INSERT INTO test_cluster (message) VALUES ('Cluster test
successful');
```

We then connect to the second node and query the table:

```
USE bookdepot;
SELECT * FROM test_cluster;
```

If the record appears on the second node, you have successfully verified that Group Replication is keeping data in sync across the cluster.

Simulating Failover

To further test high availability, you simulate a node failure. We might temporarily stop MySQL on one node:

```
sudo systemctl stop mysql
```

Then, check the cluster status on the remaining nodes:

```
SELECT * FROM performance_schema.replication_group_members;
```

We should notice that the failed node is marked as inactive or removed from the group. Once you restart the node with:

```
sudo systemctl start mysql
```

It should rejoin the cluster automatically. This exercise demonstrates the resilience of the clustered environment. With this, we successfully created a three-node cluster using MySQL Group Replication, ensuring high availability for our GitforGits application.

Configure Non-Clustered Setups

While a clustered configuration provides high availability and load balancing, a non-clustered setup can be ideal for scenarios where simplicity, lower overhead, or specific performance optimizations are required.

In a non-clustered setup, you operate with a single MySQL instance rather than a group of nodes working in tandem. This configuration typically results in reduced complexity, lower resource consumption for inter-node communication, and simpler management. However, it may also present challenges related to high availability and failover, which are automatically handled in a clustered environment. We are required to optimize the standalone instance by focusing on performance parameters such as memory allocation, disk I/O, query optimization, and network throughput. Metrics like response time, throughput, and resource utilization will be closely monitored and compared to those in a clustered setup.

Tuning Server Parameters

We begin by optimizing the InnoDB buffer pool size. To do this, first open our MySQL configuration file and adjust the following:

```
[mysqld]
```

```
innodb_buffer_pool_size = 6G
```

In the above, you allocate 6GB for caching data and indexes, which enhances query performance by reducing disk I/O.

Next, you focus on parameters that directly affect query execution. Adjusting the **query_cache_size** and **query_cache_type** can be beneficial in certain workloads. However, if our workload is highly transactional, you might choose to disable the query cache:

```
query_cache_size = 0
query_cache_type = 0
```

We also examine settings like **join_buffer_size** and **sort_buffer_size** to optimize operations that involve large table joins or sorting. For example:

```
join_buffer_size = 4M
sort_buffer_size = 2M
```

Optimizing Disk I/O and Storage

Since disk I/O can become a bottleneck, you are tuning InnoDB settings to maximize performance. We adjust parameters such as **innodb_log_file_size** and **innodb_flush_method** to ensure efficient disk writes:

```
innodb_log_file_size = 512M
innodb_flush_method = O_DIRECT
```

The larger log file size helps reduce the frequency of checkpoints, while using **O_DIRECT** minimizes the double buffering overhead, both of which are vital when a single server handles all transactional loads.

Network and Connection Settings

Sometimes, we may experience spikes in connection attempts that a single instance must handle. So, we increase the **max_connections** parameter to support higher loads:

```
max_connections = 300
```

This setting ensures that even during peak times, our single instance can manage a large number of concurrent connections without performance degradation.

We also consider adjustments to network-related settings to reduce latency like we tune

max_allowed_packet to ensure that large queries or data transfers do not cause delays:

```
max_allowed_packet = 64M
```

Implementing Monitoring and Maintenance

There are tools like MySQL Enterprise Monitor, Percona Monitoring and Management (PMM), and even simple scripts using the MySQL Performance Schema that can give you insights into query performance, buffer pool hit rates, connection usage, and disk I/O. We can set up alerts to notify you when metrics exceed predefined thresholds.

For example, you might monitor the following:

```
SHOW GLOBAL STATUS LIKE 'Innodb_buffer_pool_hit%';
SHOW GLOBAL STATUS LIKE 'Threads_connected';
```

We can also schedule tasks such as index rebuilding, table optimization, and periodic configuration reviews. Another what we could do is to automate regular backups to safeguard against data loss. These maintenance tasks ensure that our instance remains optimized and responsive over time.

While doing all this, we have very well recognized that while a clustered setup offers high availability and load balancing, a non-clustered system can deliver excellent performance when optimized correctly. It is essential to balance the increased efficiency of a single-node system with the potential risks of concentrated resource usage.

Tune Resource Allocation

No matter if your system is clustered or non-clustered, you've got to keep a close eye on memory, CPU, disk I/O, and network usage. Now, we are going to explore practical techniques and tools to monitor these performance metrics and adjust configurations dynamically.

Resource Metrics Overview

You've got a few things to keep in mind before making adjustments: first, understand the key performance metrics. We will be looking into how MySQL uses memory, CPU, and disk I/O during normal operations. It's important to note that the amount of memory allocated, especially for the InnoDB buffer pool, has a direct impact on query speed and disk access. You are also aware that CPU usage affects how quickly queries are processed, and disk I/O influences data read/write speeds.

Monitoring with Built-In Tools

Using Performance Schema and Sys Schema

We log into our MySQL shell and enable the Performance Schema, which collects detailed data on server performance:

```
SHOW VARIABLES LIKE 'performance_schema';
```

We ensure that Performance Schema is enabled so that you can access metrics such as buffer pool hit ratios, query response times, and thread activity. Additionally, you explore the Sys Schema, which provides simplified views of Performance Schema data. For example, you run:

```
SELECT * FROM sys.metrics WHERE variable_name LIKE
'innodb_buffer_pool%';
```

This query gives you insight into how effectively the buffer pool is being used. We then review other metrics like:

```
SELECT * FROM sys.host_summary;
```

This view helps you gauge overall system load, including CPU and I/O usage, which are crucial for resource planning.

Leveraging External Monitoring Tools

In addition to MySQL's built-in tools, you set up external monitoring using tools like **htop**, **iostat**, and **vmstat** on our Ubuntu system. We run:

```
htop
```

to observe CPU usage, memory consumption, and running processes in real time. We also use:

```
iostat -x 1
```

to monitor disk I/O performance, and:

```
vmstat 1
```

to track overall system performance. These tools correlate MySQL-specific metrics with the underlying system's resource utilization.

Tuning Memory Allocation

Adjusting InnoDB Buffer Pool

Since the InnoDB buffer pool benefits in caching data and indexes, you fine-tune its size based on available system memory. We open the MySQL configuration file and modify the following parameter:

```
[mysqld]
innodb_buffer_pool_size = 6G
```

In the above, you allocate 6GB for the buffer pool, which is an adjustment made after analyzing our workload through the Performance Schema. We restart the MySQL service to apply changes:

```
sudo systemctl restart mysql
```

After restarting, you re-run performance queries to ensure that the buffer pool hit rate has improved, checking with:

```
SELECT VARIABLE_VALUE
FROM performance_schema.global_status
WHERE VARIABLE_NAME = 'Innodb_buffer_pool_read_hits';
```

Fine-Tuning Other Memory Settings

We also adjust other memory settings like **`query_cache_size`** (if applicable), **`sort_buffer_size`**, and **`join_buffer_size`** to optimize how temporary data is handled during complex queries. For example:

```
sort_buffer_size = 2M
join_buffer_size = 4M
```

These adjustments control the sorting and join operations to avoid excessively consume memory, balancing overall system performance.

Managing CPU Utilization

Configuring Connection and Thread Settings

We know that CPU usage can spike during heavy transactional periods. To manage this, you adjust the **`max_connections`** and **`thread_cache_size`** parameters. In our configuration file, you set:

```
max_connections = 300
thread_cache_size = 50
```

These settings efficiently manage many simultaneous connections while reducing the overhead of creating new threads repeatedly. After modifying these parameters, you restart the MySQL service and use the following command to check active threads:

```
SHOW STATUS LIKE 'Threads_connected';
```

This helps you verify that the system is handling connections within acceptable limits.

Query Optimization Impact on CPU

We also focus on optimizing queries to reduce unnecessary CPU cycles. We review slow queries using:

```
SHOW GLOBAL STATUS LIKE 'Slow_queries';
```

and adjust query structures or add indexes where needed. Efficient query execution directly reduces CPU load, and you ensure that our tuning efforts on indexes (discussed in previous chapters) work in harmony with CPU resource allocation.

Disk I/O and Storage Tuning

Disk I/O is another critical component of resource allocation. We tune the InnoDB log file size and flush method to minimize disk write latency. In our configuration file, you adjust:

```
innodb_log_file_size = 512M

innodb_flush_method = O_DIRECT
```

These settings help improve write performance, especially under heavy transactional workloads. We monitor the impact on disk I/O with **iostat** and adjust if necessary.

Although a configuration change, you ensure that our data directory is located on high-performance storage. If possible, you configure our system to use RAID or SSDs, which can significantly reduce disk I/O bottlenecks.

Automating Resource Monitoring

To make monitoring more efficient, you develop custom scripts that periodically query resource metrics from MySQL and the operating system. For example, you create a bash script to log InnoDB buffer pool statistics:

```
#!/bin/bash
```

```
mysql -u root -pYourPassword -e "SELECT VARIABLE_NAME,
VARIABLE_VALUE FROM performance_schema.global_status WHERE
VARIABLE_NAME LIKE 'Innodb_buffer_pool%'" >>
/var/log/mysql_buffer_pool.log
```

We schedule this script via a cron job to run every five minutes:

```
sudo crontab -e
```

Add the following line:

```
*/5 * * * * /path/to/your/script.sh
```

This script automates the collection of key performance data to track trends over time and quickly identify when resource allocation adjustments are necessary.

Benchmarking and Iterative Tuning

To validate our tuning efforts, you perform benchmark tests simulating typical workloads for the GitforGits application. We use tools like sysbench to generate load and measure response times. For example:

```
sysbench --test=oltp_read_write --mysql-host=127.0.0.1 --
mysql-port=3306 --mysql-user=root --mysql-
password=YourPassword --oltp-table-size=100000 --max-time=60 -
-max-requests=0 run
```

We analyze the output, focusing on metrics such as transactions per second, query response times, and resource utilization. These benchmarks help you understand the impact of our resource allocation changes and identify any further tuning needs. Based on benchmark results and monitoring data, you make iterative adjustments to our configuration. If you notice that CPU usage remains high, you revisit query optimization or adjust thread settings. If memory usage is consistently high, you consider increasing the InnoDB buffer pool further or fine-tuning temporary table sizes.

Summary

During this chapter, we learned more about deploying and scaling MySQL instances by looking at a number of real-world configurations. We started by setting up a single-node instance on Ubuntu, where we configured essential parameters, established security measures, and verified system functionality. Then we learned how to effectively separate workloads by setting up separate data directories and custom configuration files for each instance running on the same machine.

We continued the process by implementing clustered deployments with MySQL Group Replication, which taught us how to achieve high availability and load balancing. We set up a multi-node cluster, configured replication settings, and validated data consistency across nodes through practical exercises. In parallel, we examined non-clustered setups where performance-oriented configurations were applied to a standalone instance. We adjusted memory allocation, disk I/O settings, and network parameters while monitoring key performance metrics.

We also worked on fine-tuning resource allocation by using built-in tools and third-party monitoring programs to keep an eye on how much memory, CPU, and disk space was being used. We made small changes to our configurations over and over again based on benchmark tests to make sure they worked best for a wide range of workloads. In general, we learned how to set up, manage, and expand MySQL 9 instances, and we built a strong base for meeting the operational needs of the GitforGits application.

CHAPTER 5: SECURE THE APPLICATION

Overview

This chapter teaches you various ways to protect our application, which will keep our GitforGits application safe from hackers and other people who shouldn't have access to our data. We will replace old security measures with stronger, more effective ones that use advanced plugins like caching_sha2_password to verify user identities and strong authentication methods. We will also define and apply role-based access control, allowing you to assign and manage privileges dynamically based on user attributes. So that no one on the team accidentally or maliciously misuses data, this process will make sure that everyone has the right level of access. We will also learn how to use AES_ENCRYPT() to keep private data safe while it is being sent or stored.

We will encrypt private data, learn how to decrypt it safely, and understand how important key management is for keeping data integrity through hands-on exercises. Throughout this chapter, you will be shown how to implement these security measures step by step. This will create a complete security framework that will protect our MySQL environment and our application as a whole.

Implement Strong Authentication

We get that it's super important to stop unauthorized users from getting into our database. This helps prevent data breaches and other bad stuff. By having strong authentication protocols in place, we make sure that only real users can connect to our MySQL instance. This security measure doesn't just keep your data safe; it also makes the whole system more reliable. These days, using simple passwords alone just isn't enough. We need to use advanced methods that use strong encryption and efficient caching mechanisms.

To address it, we implement caching_sha2_password, a modern authentication plugin provided by MySQL 9. This plugin leverages SHA-256 hashing combined with caching techniques to enhance security and reduce connection overhead. It offers several advantages over older authentication methods like mysql_native_password, including stronger encryption and improved resistance to dictionary and brute-force attacks.

To implement, following the below steps:

Verify Plugin Availability

We begin by verifying that caching_sha2_password is available on our MySQL 9 instance. After logging into the MySQL shell:

```
mysql -u root -p
```

we run the command:

```
SHOW PLUGINS;
```

We check the output to confirm that caching_sha2_password is listed and active.

Create a User with Strong Authentication

Next, we create a new user using caching_sha2_password to secure access by executing:

```
CREATE USER 'bookadmin'@'%' IDENTIFIED WITH
caching_sha2_password BY 'YourStrongPassword!';
```

Doing this, we set up the user bookadmin with a strong password that adheres to our security policies.

Grant Necessary Privileges

After creating the user, we grant the required privileges so that bookadmin can manage our GitforGits application effectively. For this, we execute:

```
GRANT ALL PRIVILEGES ON *.* TO 'bookadmin'@'%' WITH GRANT
OPTION;
FLUSH PRIVILEGES;
```

These commands ensure that the new user has the appropriate level of access and that all changes are applied immediately.

Testing Authentication

To confirm that caching_sha2_password is functioning correctly, we log out of the MySQL shell and then log in again using the new credentials:

```
mysql -u bookadmin -p
```

Upon entering the strong password, we observe that the login is successful and the connection is secured using caching_sha2_password.

Configuring Client Connections

We also verify that our client applications and connectors are compatible with caching_sha2_password. Most modern MySQL drivers support this plugin, but you should check our application's configuration. If needed, update connection strings to ensure that they use the new authentication method. This step maintains a seamless integration between our application and the secure MySQL instance.

Apply Role-Based Access Control

Recent innovations in RBAC have introduced the capability to automatically assign roles based on user attributes such as department, job function, or even behavioral metrics. We see that these advancements allow for a more granular and dynamic control over database access. Instead of manually assigning roles to each user, automated systems evaluate user profiles and assign roles accordingly.

For instance, if a user belongs to the sales team, the system can automatically grant them access to order and customer data, while restricting access to sensitive administrative tables. This mechanism reduces the risk of misconfigured privileges and ensures consistency across the system. To implemenet it, follow the below steps:

Define Roles and Privileges

We start by outlining the key roles required for our GitforGits application. For example, common roles might include:

- **Admin:** Full access to all database operations and configurations.
- **Manager:** Access to sales data, order processing, and inventory control.
- **Sales:** Limited access focused on order creation and customer interaction.
- **Support:** Read-only access to customer information and order histories.

We work with our team to document these roles and their associated permissions. Each role is defined with a clear set of privileges that align with the job functions. For example, the Admin role may have permissions to create, modify, and drop tables, while the Sales role may only have permissions to insert and select data from certain tables.

Create Roles in MySQL

We can create roles using the **CREATE ROLE** statement. For this, we proceed by executing commands to define each role:

```
CREATE ROLE 'admin_role';
CREATE ROLE 'manager_role';
CREATE ROLE 'sales_role';
CREATE ROLE 'support_role';
```

After defining these roles, we assign specific privileges to them. For instance, to grant full privileges to the admin_role on all databases, you run:

```
GRANT ALL PRIVILEGES ON *.* TO 'admin_role';
```

Similarly, for a role that has read-only access, such as support_role, you execute:

```
GRANT SELECT ON bookdepot.* TO 'support_role';
```

We continue by mapping out the privileges for each role, ensuring that the permission sets align with the business requirements of the project.

Automate Role Assignment

To implement automated role assignment, you use MySQL's ability to incorporate user attributes in role management. Although MySQL does not natively support attribute-based role assignment out-of-the-box like some enterprise identity providers, you can simulate this functionality using stored procedures or scheduled events.

Assuming that we maintain a table called **user_profiles** with columns such as **username**, **department**, and **job_title**. SO here, we create a stored procedure to assign roles based on the department:

```
DELIMITER $$
CREATE PROCEDURE assign_user_roles()
BEGIN
    DECLARE done INT DEFAULT FALSE;
    DECLARE uname VARCHAR(100);
    DECLARE dept VARCHAR(50);
    DECLARE cur CURSOR FOR SELECT username, department FROM
user_profiles;
    DECLARE CONTINUE HANDLER FOR NOT FOUND SET done = TRUE;

    OPEN cur;
    read_loop: LOOP
        FETCH cur INTO uname, dept;
        IF done THEN
            LEAVE read_loop;
        END IF;

        IF dept = 'Sales' THEN
```

```
            GRANT 'sales_role' TO uname;
        ELSEIF dept = 'Management' THEN
            GRANT 'manager_role' TO uname;
        ELSEIF dept = 'IT' THEN
            GRANT 'admin_role' TO uname;
        ELSE
            GRANT 'support_role' TO uname;
        END IF;
    END LOOP;
    CLOSE cur;
    FLUSH PRIVILEGES;
END$$
DELIMITER ;
```

In this procedure, we loop through each user profile and assign roles based on their department. We can schedule this procedure to run periodically to keep role assignments up-to-date with any changes in user attributes.

Testing and Validation

Next, we verify the roles granted to a specific user by executing:

```
SHOW GRANTS FOR 'some_user'@'%';
```

This command lets you review whether the correct privileges have been applied. Additionally, you simulate scenarios by inserting test data into the **`user_profiles`** table and manually invoking the stored procedure:

```
CALL assign_user_roles();
```

After running the procedure, you check the roles of the test users to confirm that the assignments reflect their department or job attributes.

Refinement and Best Practices

We understand that the automated role assignment mechanism might need refinement over time. Additionally, you may consider integrating external identity providers in the future, which can offer more advanced attribute-based access control features.

We also set up monitoring and logging for role changes. For instance, you can enable audit logging in MySQL to track changes in user privileges:

```
SET GLOBAL audit_log_policy = 'ALL';
```

This setting helps you maintain a record of role assignments and modifications, which is essential for compliance and security audits.

Throughout this process, we combined the strengths of MySQL's native RBAC features with custom automation to simulate advanced attribute-based access control. By creating roles, mapping privileges, and automating role assignment via stored procedures, we achieved a flexible and scalable security framework.

Encrypt Data with AES_ENCRYPT()

AES, or Advanced Encryption Standard, is a pretty solid encryption algorithm. It's used a lot in MySQL 9, and it basically takes plaintext and turns it into ciphertext. With AES, you only need one key to encrypt and decrypt, which makes managing the key super important for security. The main perk of using AES_ENCRYPT() is that it gives you a built-in, simple way to protect your data without needing extra libraries.If you encrypt sensitive stuff like user credentials, financial data, or personal information, you can lower the risk of exposure if the database gets hacked.

Encrypting Data at Rest

When securing data at rest, our objective is to store data in an encrypted format on disk so that unauthorized users cannot read it even if they gain access to the physical files or backup media. For this, we begin by creating a table that will store sensitive information. Think of a table named **customer_info** that holds customer details, including a confidential field such as **ssn** (Social Security Number).

Creating a Sample Table with Encrypted Data

Here, we create the table in our GitforGits application using AES_ENCRYPT() to encrypt the sensitive column:

```
CREATE TABLE customer_info (
    customer_id INT AUTO_INCREMENT PRIMARY KEY,
    name VARCHAR(255) NOT NULL,
    email VARCHAR(255),
    ssn VARBINARY(255)
```

```
) ENGINE=InnoDB;
```

In the above, the **ssn** column is defined as VARBINARY to store the binary output of the AES_ENCRYPT() function.

Inserting Encrypted Data

We then insert data into the table, encrypting the **ssn** field on insertion. To achieve this, we use AES_ENCRYPT() along with a secret key. The secret key is a critical element that should be managed securely:

```
SET @key_str = 'My$ecretKey123';
INSERT INTO customer_info (name, email, ssn)
VALUES (
    'Alice Smith',
    'alice@gitforgits.com',
    AES_ENCRYPT('123-45-6789', @key_str)
);
```

In the above sample program, the plain-text SSN **'123-45-6789'** is encrypted using **@key_str** and stored in the table. We note that the key should not be hard-coded in production; instead, it should be securely stored and managed.

Retrieving and Decrypting Data

To read the encrypted data, we use the AES_DECRYPT() function along with the same secret key:

```
SELECT
    customer_id,
    name,
    email,
    CAST(AES_DECRYPT(ssn, @key_str) AS CHAR(50)) AS
decrypted_ssn
FROM customer_info;
```

This query decrypts the **ssn** column, converting it back into human-readable text. We learn that proper key management is crucial because without the correct key, data cannot be decrypted.

Encrypting Data in Transit

While MySQL provides native support for encrypted connections via SSL/TLS, there are scenarios where additional application-level encryption using AES_ENCRYPT() is beneficial. For instance, if you need to ensure that sensitive data remains encrypted when transferred between servers or stored temporarily in caches, using AES_ENCRYPT() adds an extra layer of security.

Encrypting Data Before Transmission

We simulate encrypting data before sending it over the network. Consider a scenario where sensitive order details need to be transmitted securely between different modules of our GitforGits Book Depot application. We can use AES_ENCRYPT() to encrypt such details, ensuring that even if intercepted, the data remains protected.

```
SET @order_key = 'Order$ecretKey456';
INSERT INTO orders (customer_id, order_date, total_amount, encrypted_details)
VALUES (
    1,
    NOW(),
    99.95,
    AES_ENCRYPT('Sensitive order details: Credit Card Info', @order_key)
);
```

In this command, the **encrypted_details** field is used to store encrypted order information.

Decrypting Data After Reception

Once the data is received by the intended module, it can be decrypted using the same key:

```
SELECT
    order_id,
    customer_id,
    order_date,
    total_amount,
```

```
    CAST(AES_DECRYPT(encrypted_details, @order_key) AS
CHAR(255)) AS decrypted_details
FROM orders;
```

This query allows the recipient system to retrieve and decrypt the order details, ensuring that sensitive information is only accessible to authorized components of the application.

Throughout this process, we learned several key best practices:

- The secret key used in AES_ENCRYPT() is fundamental to data security. In our project, we ensure that keys are stored securely, possibly using environment variables or dedicated key management systems rather than embedding them directly in our SQL scripts.
- When storing encrypted data, always use appropriate data types such as VARBINARY to accommodate the binary output of AES_ENCRYPT(). This avoids data truncation or encoding issues.
- Ensure that both encryption and decryption operations consistently use the same secret key and encryption mode. Any mismatch will lead to failed decryption attempts.
- While AES_ENCRYPT() secures data at rest and in transit at the application level, it should be used in conjunction with other security measures such as SSL/TLS for network connections and robust access control policies.
- Be mindful of the performance overhead associated with encryption and decryption operations, especially in high-transaction environments. Benchmark our system and adjust our configurations to strike the right balance between security and performance.

Summary

One way we learned more about how to keep our MySQL environment safe was by using several layers to protect our GitforGits application's important data. When we first set up our system, we used caching_sha2_password to make sure that only people who were supposed to be there could get in. We made sure our authentication methods were strong enough to keep our instance safe by setting up and creating secure user accounts and doing exercises.

After that, we worked on controlling access based on roles. We defined roles like admin, manager, sales, and support, and set up automated systems to assign these roles to users based on how they behave. At the same time, we looked at AES_ENCRYPT() and AES_DECRYPT() for data encryption. We learned how to secretly encode private information while it's being sent or stored, changing it from plain text to ciphertext, which can't be read. Throughout the chapter, we covered best practices for key management and continuous monitoring to ensure a strong security posture.

Chapter 6: Establish High Availability and Replication

Overview

In this chapter, you will learn how to make a reliable and expandable database environment for our GitforGits application, which covers high availability and replication. To begin, you will learn the basics of replication, such as how to make sure that work is spread out evenly and replicate data across multiple servers for backup purposes. The more you learn, the better replication techniques you will learn, such as intelligent data filtering and Change Data Capture.

We will also set up a multimaster-slave replication system so that more than one node can write at the same time. If you use this method, our system will be able to keep running even if one node fails. We will also use MySQL InnoDB Cluster and MySQL Router to set up failover strategies that will make sure the system can automatically promote a new primary node in case of problems. As you go through this chapter, real-life examples and configurations will help you plan, set up, and run a highly available MySQL environment that works for our app.

Replication Basics

Replication lets you make copies of your main database on other servers. These extra servers, also called "replicas," get updates from the main one, so everything is updated at the same time. We've found that this setup not only makes data more available but also helps balance the workload for things that need to be read a lot. Since the workload is spread across different servers, replication makes the whole system work better and better.

Following are some of the latest and the advanced aspects of Replication:

Change Data Capture (CDC)

We are examining Change Data Capture, a modern replication technique that tracks and records changes in the source database in real time. CDC enables us to stream updates to replicas or external systems with minimal latency, ensuring that our data synchronization is as current as possible. We will see how CDC can be integrated into our replication strategy to efficiently propagate changes.

Materialized Views

Materialized views are another advanced concept that you will explore. They allow us to store precomputed query results for faster access and can be automatically updated through replication. In our project, materialized views can be used to optimize complex queries by providing quick access to aggregated data without repeatedly computing it from scratch.

Multi-Master and Peer-to-Peer Replication

We will also learn about multi-master replication, where multiple servers act as primary nodes and can accept write operations. This setup provides redundancy and improves availability, though it requires conflict resolution strategies. Peer-to-peer replication extends this concept by allowing each node to function equally, sharing updates among themselves. Both configurations support high availability and ensure that no single point of failure exists in our GitforGits system.

Geo-Replication and Data Locality Optimization

We introduce geo-replication, which distributes copies of the database across different geographical regions. This method reduces latency for users by serving data from a location closer to them and ensures data remains accessible even during regional outages. Data locality optimization goes hand in hand with geo-replication, as it allows us to fine-tune where data is stored and accessed based on user location, enhancing the overall performance and user experience.

Asynchronous Replication with Conflict Detection

Asynchronous replication is commonly used to replicate data without waiting for the primary server to confirm the transaction. We will learn how this mode improves performance by allowing the primary to process transactions quickly, while the replica updates lag slightly behind. In this model, conflict detection is crucial to identify and resolve discrepancies that might occur due to latency, ensuring data integrity across the system.

Snapshot Isolation

Snapshot isolation is another advanced feature that you will explore. It provides a consistent view of the data by taking a "snapshot" of the database at a specific point in time, allowing transactions to proceed without being affected by concurrent changes. This isolation level is particularly useful in environments with high levels of concurrent transactions, as it prevents conflicts and maintains consistency across replicas.

Intelligent Data Filtering

Finally, we delve into intelligent data filtering, a modern technique that allows you to replicate only a subset of the data based on specific criteria. This method is useful when only certain parts of the database need to be synchronized with remote systems or analytical platforms. By filtering data intelligently, you reduce unnecessary network load and storage usage, while still ensuring that the most critical information is always available where it is needed.

We plan to combine all these techniques to create a comprehensive replication strategy. For example, we might implement asynchronous replication with conflict detection on a multi-master setup, then integrate CDC to capture real-time changes and use intelligent data filtering to minimize overhead. These advanced features work together to ensure that our data remains consistent and readily available, regardless of the operational demands or network conditions.

Setup Multi Master-Slave Replication

Understanding Multi Master-Slave Replication

We get that a standard master-slave setup has one main server for writing and one or more secondary servers for reading. But a multi-master setup lets you have a bunch of nodes accept writing transactions. It's a pretty cool way to boost availability, load distribution, and redundancy. With multiple masters, you're less likely to have downtime and get better performance by spreading out the writing workload across a few nodes.

We begin by exploring the benefits of a multi master-slave configuration compared to the traditional master-slave model. In a simple master-slave setup, if the primary server fails, write operations come to a halt until a new master is promoted. In contrast, multi master-slave replication allows several servers to act as masters, each capable of processing write transactions. This not only ensures continuous availability but also distributes the load more evenly across the system. Additionally, this configuration supports higher scalability and fault tolerance. With multiple masters, you can handle high volumes of write operations, and in case one node goes down, others can continue processing transactions without significant disruption.

Configuring Masters

Before getting into the specifics, we are planning out the multi-master-slave environment for our GitforGits application. We're going with a setup where there are two master nodes that both accept write operations and at least one slave node that replicates data from both masters. We're making sure that network latency is kept to a minimum between nodes and confirming that each server is running MySQL 9 with the necessary replication parameters enabled. Our aim is to set up a balanced system where data is consistent and we've got strategies in place for dealing with conflicts when different masters are writing at the same time.

Update and Configure Master Nodes

On each master node, we start by ensuring that the MySQL configuration file is set up to support multi master replication. First, open the configuration file on each master and make the following adjustments:

```
[mysqld]
server_id = 1  # For the first master, and a unique number for the second master (e.g., 2)
log_bin = mysql-bin
binlog_format = ROW
gtid_mode = ON
enforce_gtid_consistency = ON
master_info_repository = TABLE
```

```
relay_log_info_repository = TABLE
transaction_write_set_extraction = XXHASH64
```

Here we need to assign a unique **server_id** to each master. We also set **gtid_mode** to ON and enforce GTID consistency, which simplifies tracking transactions across multiple masters.

Create a Replication User on Each Master

Next, we create a replication user on each master node that will be used by the slave(s) to connect and replicate data. Next, we log into each master's MySQL shell and run:

```
CREATE USER 'repl'@'%' IDENTIFIED WITH caching_sha2_password
BY 'StrongReplicatePass!';
GRANT REPLICATION SLAVE ON *.* TO 'repl'@'%';
FLUSH PRIVILEGES;
```

This user will be common across nodes and will facilitate secure and consistent replication.

Configuring Slave

Setup Slave Node

On the slave node, we modify the MySQL configuration file to designate it as a replication recipient. Open **/etc/mysql/mysql.conf.d/mysqld.cnf** on the slave and add the following:

```
[mysqld]
server_id = 3  # Ensure this is unique among all nodes
relay_log = /var/log/mysql/mysql-relay-bin.log
log_bin = mysql-bin
binlog_format = ROW
gtid_mode = ON
enforce_gtid_consistency = ON
```

The slave's **server_id** should be different from those of the masters. The relay log is essential for processing transactions from multiple sources.

Configure Slave to Connect to Both Masters

Since our slave needs to replicate from two master nodes, we configure it to connect to each master using GTIDs. On the slave's MySQL shell, set up replication channels for each master. First, stop any existing replication threads:

```
STOP SLAVE;
RESET SLAVE ALL;
```

Then, configure the first replication channel:

```
CHANGE MASTER TO
  MASTER_HOST='master1_ip',
  MASTER_USER='repl',
  MASTER_PASSWORD='StrongReplicatePass!',
  MASTER_PORT=3306,
  MASTER_AUTO_POSITION=1,
  MASTER_CONNECT_RETRY=10
FOR CHANNEL 'master1';
```

Next, configure the second replication channel:

```
CHANGE MASTER TO
  MASTER_HOST='master2_ip',
  MASTER_USER='repl',
  MASTER_PASSWORD='StrongReplicatePass!',
  MASTER_PORT=3306,
  MASTER_AUTO_POSITION=1,
  MASTER_CONNECT_RETRY=10
FOR CHANNEL 'master2';
```

Make sure to replace **master1_ip** and **master2_ip** with the actual IP addresses of our master nodes.

Start Replication Channels

After configuring both channels, start the slave threads:

```
START SLAVE FOR CHANNEL 'master1';
```

```
START SLAVE FOR CHANNEL 'master2';
```

We then verify that the replication channels are running smoothly:

```
SHOW SLAVE STATUS FOR CHANNEL 'master1'\G
SHOW SLAVE STATUS FOR CHANNEL 'master2'\G
```

Finally, we review the output to ensure that the **`Slave_IO_Running`** and **`Slave_SQL_Running`** statuses are set to **`Yes`** for both channels. This confirms that the slave is receiving and processing transactions from both masters.

Conflict Detection and Resolution

When you've got a multi-master environment, you might run into write conflicts—that's when two masters update the same data at the same time. We've got strategies to spot and fix these conflicts. MySQL 9 uses GTIDs to detect conflicts, since they track transactions in a unique way across all nodes. We make sure our applications are set up to minimize conflicts by carefully partitioning data or using application-level logic to handle any discrepancies.

In our setup, we keep an eye on conflict logs and set up alerts to spot conflicts when they pop up. We're also thinking about using triggers or stored procedures to automatically resolve conflicts, but these solutions need to be tailored to fit specific business logic requirements.

Testing Multi Master-Slave Environment

Insert Data on both Masters

To verify that our multi master-slave configuration works as expected, we perform tests by inserting data into both master nodes. On master node 1, we execute:

```
USE bookdepot;

INSERT INTO orders (customer_id, order_date, total_amount)
VALUES (1, NOW(), 49.99);
```

On master node 2, we execute:

```
USE bookdepot;

INSERT INTO orders (customer_id, order_date, total_amount)
VALUES (2, NOW(), 79.95);
```

Verify Replication on Slave

After inserting data on both masters, we connect to the slave and verify that the data from both masters is replicated correctly:

```
USE bookdepot;
SELECT * FROM orders;
```

We should see entries from both master nodes. This confirms that the slave is successfully replicating data from multiple sources. Also, we continuously monitor the replication channels by reviewing logs and using the **SHOW SLAVE STATUS** command.

Throughout this process, we adopt several best practices to ensure a robust multi master-slave setup:

- Each node is assigned a unique server ID to avoid replication conflicts.
- Using GTIDs simplifies replication management and conflict detection.
- We schedule frequent backups to safeguard against data loss in case of replication failures.
- Integrating monitoring tools allows us to track replication performance and detect issues early.
- Where possible, data partitioning or application-level controls are used to minimize the likelihood of write conflicts.

This configuration allows multiple master nodes to process write operations concurrently, reducing the risk of downtime and distributing the workload more evenly. Our slave node effectively aggregates data from both masters, ensuring that all changes are synchronized and available for read operations.

Advanced Replication Options

We're expanding our replication strategy in this section by using advanced techniques like CDC and Intelligent Data Filtering. These methods are designed to improve replication performance and make sure our GitforGits application works efficiently under heavy workloads.

Implementing CDC

CDC is a technique that monitors and captures changes in the source database, such as insertions, updates, and deletions, and then streams these changes to replica nodes in real time. This method minimizes latency and ensures that our replicas remain as current as possible without needing full table scans or frequent bulk transfers. We learn that CDC is particularly beneficial in high-transaction environments, where capturing every change quickly can significantly enhance replication performance.

In our GitforGits application, we implement CDC by using MySQL's binary log (binlog) feature, which records all transactions that modify data. We configure the binlog to operate in ROW format, as it captures the actual data changes rather than just the SQL statements:

```
[mysqld]
log_bin = mysql-bin
binlog_format = ROW
gtid_mode = ON
enforce_gtid_consistency = ON
transaction_write_set_extraction = XXHASH64
```

We ensure that these settings are included in the configuration file on all replication nodes. With CDC enabled through the binlog, any change made on the primary server is recorded and immediately available for replication. This setup minimizes the lag between the primary and its replicas, ensuring that our application always works with the most up-to-date data.

We can also integrate CDC with external tools that can consume binlog events for advanced processing. For example, we can use a CDC tool like Debezium to stream changes from our MySQL instance into a Kafka cluster for real-time analytics or additional processing, that will allow us to build a robust pipeline where changes in our GitforGits Book Depot database trigger immediate downstream actions, such as updating a search index or notifying other systems of critical updates.

Implementing Intelligent Data Filtering

Next, we focus on Intelligent Data Filtering, an advanced technique that enables us to replicate only a subset of data based on predefined criteria. In many scenarios, not all data in the source database needs to be replicated. By filtering out unnecessary data, we reduce replication load, minimize network traffic, and improve the speed at which essential data is synchronized.

In our GitforGits application, we set up intelligent data filtering by leveraging MySQL replication filters. These filters allow us to include or exclude databases, tables, or even specific rows based on conditions. We edit the MySQL configuration file on our replication nodes to include filter options.

For example, if we want to replicate only order-related tables from a larger database, we might specify:

```
[mysqld]
replicate-do-db=bookdepot_orders
```

Alternatively, if our scenario requires more granular control, we can use row-based filters implemented via custom triggers or stored procedures to mark records for replication. Suppose we have a table that stores both critical order data and ancillary log data; we could design a mechanism where only records with a specific flag are eligible for replication. Imagine our **orders** table contains a column named **replicate_flag** that indicates whether a row should be replicated. We can set up a trigger that automatically sets this flag based on business logic as below:

```
DELIMITER $$
CREATE TRIGGER set_replicate_flag BEFORE INSERT ON orders
FOR EACH ROW
BEGIN
    IF NEW.total_amount > 0 THEN
        SET NEW.replicate_flag = 1;
    ELSE
        SET NEW.replicate_flag = 0;
    END IF;
END$$
DELIMITER ;
```

With this trigger in place, only rows with **replicate_flag** equal to 1 are flagged for replication. We then modify our replication filters (using custom replication channels or middleware solutions) to process only the rows meeting this criterion.

Here, we observed that intelligent filtering minimizes replication overhead by ensuring that only essential data is transferred to replicas. This not only improves replication speed but also reduces storage requirements on replica servers. Moreover, by filtering data intelligently, we can tailor the replicated dataset to the specific needs of different application components. For instance, if a reporting server requires only summary data, intelligent filtering can exclude granular transactional details, thereby streamlining query performance and reducing resource consumption.

Both of these strategies help make our MySQL environment more resilient and scalable, and they also help make our GitforGits application more efficient. These advanced techniques help us support high transaction volumes and dynamic data requirements in a modern, distributed database system.

Design Failover Strategies

Overview

Failover is a critical component of high availability systems, ensuring that if one database server fails, another can take over without causing significant downtime. We examine several failover strategies, including manual promotion of replicas, automated failover with clustering, and the use of load balancers. Among these, the most favorable solution for our project is an automated failover strategy using MySQL InnoDB Cluster. This approach combines Group Replication for data synchronization with MySQL Router to intelligently direct client connections to the healthiest node. With this setup, you ensure that write and read operations continue uninterrupted even if one or more nodes experience issues.

It is said that InnoDB Cluster provides the following benefits:

- The cluster automatically promotes another node as the primary if the current primary fails, minimizing downtime.
- Using Group Replication, the cluster maintains data consistency across all nodes, ensuring that the latest transactions are available across the board.
- MySQL Router manages client connections, dynamically routing traffic to the active primary, so you do not need to manually update connection strings or configuration settings.
- The system scales by adding more nodes, which can also serve read workloads, thereby improving overall performance.

Setting Up MySQL InnoDB Cluster

Configure Cluster Nodes

We begin by configuring each node in our InnoDB Cluster. Each node must have MySQL 9 installed and be configured with Group Replication settings. On each node, you ensure that the configuration file includes the following parameters:

```
[mysqld]
server_id = <unique_id>
log_bin = mysql-bin
binlog_format = ROW
gtid_mode = ON
enforce_gtid_consistency = ON
master_info_repository = TABLE
relay_log_info_repository = TABLE
```

```
transaction_write_set_extraction = XXHASH64
loose-group_replication_local_address = "node_ip:33061"
loose-group_replication_group_seeds =
"node1_ip:33061,node2_ip:33061,node3_ip:33061"
loose-group_replication_group_name = "book_depot_cluster"
loose-group_replication_start_on_boot = ON
```

Replace **<unique_id>** and the placeholder IP addresses with the appropriate values for our environment. We verify that these settings are consistent across all nodes for proper Group Replication and cluster formation.

Bootstrapping InnoDB Cluster

Next, you need to bootstrap the InnoDB Cluster. On one node, which you designate as the initial primary, log into the MySQL shell and enable Group Replication bootstrapping:

```
SET GLOBAL group_replication_bootstrap_group=ON;
START GROUP_REPLICATION;
SET GLOBAL group_replication_bootstrap_group=OFF;
```

After bootstrapping, you confirm the cluster status by querying:

```
SELECT * FROM performance_schema.replication_group_members;
```

We should see the initial node listed as a member. Then, on the remaining nodes, simply start Group Replication:

```
START GROUP_REPLICATION;
```

Verify that all nodes have joined the cluster by checking the same query on each node. This forms our InnoDB Cluster, with multiple nodes synchronized through Group Replication.

Integrate MySQL Router

With the cluster in place, you integrate MySQL Router to manage client connections. We install MySQL Router on a separate server or on one of the cluster nodes:

```
sudo apt install mysql-router
```

After installation, configure MySQL Router by generating a configuration file that connects to our InnoDB Cluster. We run:

```
mysqlrouter --bootstrap root@primary_node_ip:3306 --
user=mysqlrouter --directory /etc/mysqlrouter
```

This command bootstraps MySQL Router with the cluster's details, generating a configuration that includes endpoints for read-write and read-only traffic. The configuration typically creates two ports: one for read-write operations and another for read-only operations.

Start and Verify MySQL Router

Once the configuration is complete, start MySQL Router:

```
sudo systemctl start mysqlrouter
```

Check the status to confirm that it is running:

```
sudo systemctl status mysqlrouter
```

Now, test the connection through MySQL Router by connecting using the MySQL client:

```
mysql -u root -p -h router_ip -P <read_write_port>
```

We should be able to perform queries as if you were connected to the primary node. MySQL Router automatically redirects our connection to the current primary, ensuring seamless access even if failover occurs.

Implementing Automated Failover

Simulate a Failover Scenario

To validate our failover strategy, you simulate a failure of the primary node. On the current primary, you stop the MySQL service:

```
sudo systemctl stop mysql
```

Within moments, the InnoDB Cluster automatically promotes one of the remaining nodes as the new primary. We then check the status from another node:

```
SELECT * FROM performance_schema.replication_group_members;
```

We verify that a new primary has been established and that replication continues without interruption.

Validate Continuous Operations

After simulating the failure, connect through MySQL Router again:

```
mysql -u root -p -h router_ip -P <read_write_port>
```

Execute a few queries to confirm that the new primary is handling the write operations as expected. This successful test demonstrates that our automated failover strategy is working correctly, ensuring continuous database operations even when a node fails.

As we implement and maintain our failover strategy, we adhere to several best practices:

- Ensure that all nodes have consistent replication and security settings.
- Each node must have a unique server ID to avoid replication conflicts.
- Even with automated failover, maintaining regular backups is essential for disaster recovery.
- Regularly test failover procedures and document any changes to the configuration or process.
- Use automated monitoring tools to detect and alert on any anomalies in real time.

This failover solution minimizes downtime, maintains data consistency, and distributes workloads efficiently across multiple nodes. Through careful configuration, simulation of failure scenarios, and ongoing monitoring, we have built a resilient database environment capable of handling disruptions without impacting user experience.

Summary

In conclusion, we learned more about database replication by using a number of advanced methods to make sure that the database was always available and that the data was always in sync. We started by going over the basics of replication and learning how it works to copy data across multiple servers for backup and load balancing. Then we moved on to more advanced features, like Change Data Capture and intelligent data filtering, which let us record changes in real time and copy only the most important data.

We kept going by setting up a multi-master-slave replication environment. This way, multiple nodes could handle write transactions at the same time, which was much more fault-tolerant and scalable than traditional master-slave models. We learned how to give each node its own server ID, make sure that GTIDs are always the same, and set up dedicated replication channels to make sure that everything in the cluster is in sync. We added more security to our system by using MySQL InnoDB Cluster and MySQL Router to set up automated failover plans. Also, we were able to simulate failures, check the status of replication, and make sure that the system could automatically promote a new primary without stopping service. Finally, we created a strong replication framework that protected the integrity of the data, kept downtime to a minimum, and offered a scalable solution that could handle a lot of transactions in a production setting.

CHAPTER 7: QUERIES PERFORMANCE AND OPTIMIZATION

Overview

This chapter will teach you the art and science of query performance and optimization. This will give you the skills to make our MySQL environment work as efficiently as possible. We will look at how to use MySQL Workbench and other monitoring tools to gather and understand key performance metrics. This will find problems and ways to make things better.

As you learn more, you will be able to use EXPLAIN to look at query execution plans, make good indexes, and change memory buffers and caches to make sure that getting data is as fast as possible. We will walk you through real-life scenarios and hands-on exercises that will improve both simple and complex SQL queries. We will also discover how to set up custom dashboards and integrate external monitoring solutions, ensuring that our database consistently performs at its peak. At the end of this chapter, you will know all the techniques and best practices you need to keep our MySQL system running smoothly and scalable so it can meet the needs of our GitforGits application.

Explore System Performance Metrics

We're going to talk about different things that show how healthy the system is, like how much CPU is being used, how much memory is being used, how much disk I/O is happening, and how long it's taking to respond to queries. Once you understand these metrics, you'll be able to spot bottlenecks and make the system more efficient.

Key Performance Metrics

CPU and Memory Utilization

We begin by examining CPU usage and memory allocation, two of the most important resources for any database system. High CPU usage might indicate inefficient queries or insufficient indexing, while memory metrics, such as the InnoDB buffer pool hit rate, reveal how well our data is cached. Monitoring these parameters can determine whether to adjust configurations like **`max_connections`**, **`innodb_buffer_pool_size`**, or thread-related settings.

Disk I/O and Latency

Next, we focus on disk I/O performance. Disk read/write speeds and latency can significantly impact query performance, especially when large datasets are involved. Key parameters include the rate of disk operations, the efficiency of the disk cache, and the performance of the InnoDB log file and flush methods. These insights allow you to decide if you need to optimize storage configurations or even consider hardware upgrades.

Query Execution and Throughput

Understanding query performance is vital. Metrics such as query execution time, slow query counts, and the number of transactions per second provide a clear picture of how efficiently our MySQL instance handles workloads. These performance indicators help in pinpointing problematic queries and determining whether additional indexes or query restructuring are needed.

Introducing MySQL Workbench

MySQL Workbench Features

To help monitor and analyze these metrics, we introduce MySQL Workbench, a powerful integrated tool designed for database design, administration, and performance optimization. MySQL Workbench offers several features that are invaluable for tracking system performance:

- MySQL Workbench provides detailed, real-time visualizations of key metrics, such as CPU usage, memory allocation, and disk I/O. These charts allow you to quickly identify trends and potential bottlenecks.
- The tool includes query profiling features that display detailed execution plans. By using the EXPLAIN command within MySQL Workbench, you can see how our queries are executed, which helps in identifying inefficient operations or missing indexes.
- MySQL Workbench lets you monitor server status, including active connections, thread usage, and replication status. These insights are crucial for understanding how well our server is handling concurrent operations.
- It integrates seamlessly with MySQL's Performance Schema, providing deeper insights into various performance metrics, such as buffer pool activity and query latency.
- We can create custom dashboards that display the metrics most relevant to our GitforGits application. These dashboards offer a centralized view of the performance data, making it easier to spot issues before they escalate.

MySQL Workbench in Practice

Here's what we will do: we will walk you through using MySQL Workbench to monitor our system. First, launch MySQL Workbench and connect to our MySQL 9 instance.In the "Server Status" section, you'll see a real-time graph of CPU and memory usage. This will show you the impact of your current workloads on system resources.

Next, navigate to the "Performance Reports" tab. In this, you review reports such as the "Top Queries" and "InnoDB Buffer Pool Efficiency." These reports provide insights into which queries consume the most resources and how effectively the InnoDB buffer pool is being utilized. For instance, if you notice that certain queries consistently rank among the slowest, you can look into further using the query profiling tool to identify opportunities for optimization.

We also explore the "Explain Plan" feature by running sample queries and examining the generated execution plans. This feature visually breaks down each query's operation, highlighting areas where indexes might be missing or where full table scans occur. Moreover, MySQL Workbench's integration with the Performance Schema enables you to drill down into detailed system metrics. We can review buffer pool statistics, connection counts, and disk I/O activity, providing a comprehensive view of our server's performance. The ability to customize dashboards means you can tailor the monitoring experience to focus on the metrics most critical to our operational needs.

Up and Running with MySQL Workbench

Now, we are going to set up MySQL Workbench in our environment. This way, we can use its awesome monitoring and diagnostic tools for our MySQL 9 instances.First, we are installing and configuring the tool, and then we will use it to collect and analyze performance metrics.

Installing MySQL Workbench

Download and Install

We begin by downloading MySQL Workbench from the official MySQL website. We open our browser and navigate to the download page for MySQL Workbench. Choose the version compatible with our operating system (Ubuntu in this case) and download the .deb package. Once the download is complete, you open the terminal and run:

```
sudo dpkg -i mysql-workbench-community_<version>_amd64.deb
```

If any dependency errors occur, you resolve them by running:

```
sudo apt-get install -f
```

This process installs MySQL Workbench on our Ubuntu machine, ensuring that you have all necessary components for its operation.

Launching MySQL Workbench

After installation, you launch MySQL Workbench from the applications menu or by executing:

```
mysql-workbench
```

Upon startup, you see the Workbench interface, which provides several options such as Database Administration, SQL Development, and Server Administration. We are now ready to connect to our MySQL 9 instance and begin monitoring performance.

Configuring MySQL Workbench

Setting up a Connection

We create a new connection to our MySQL 9 instance. In MySQL Workbench, you click on the "+" icon next to MySQL Connections. A configuration window appears, prompting you to enter connection details.

Here, we provide the following information:

- **Connection Name:** GitforGits_Instance
- **Hostname:** (e.g., 127.0.0.1 or the server's IP)
- **Port:** 3306 (or another port if customized)
- **Username:** root or another administrative user
- **Password:** (you can store the password securely)

After entering these details, you click "Test Connection" to ensure that the connection is successful. Once confirmed, you save the connection and proceed.

Configuring Preferences

Within MySQL Workbench, we adjust preferences to optimize our monitoring experience. We navigate to the "Edit" menu and select "Preferences." Under the "SQL Editor" and "Performance" sections, you configure options such as query timeout settings, font sizes for readability, and default behaviors for query execution.

Collecting Performance Metrics

Accessing Server Status and Dashboard

Now that our connection is set up, you click on the "Server Status" tab in MySQL Workbench. This dashboard displays real-time metrics such as CPU usage, memory allocation, and disk I/O. We observe graphs that represent the current load on the MySQL server. These visualizations help us understand the immediate state of our system and pinpoint potential resource bottlenecks.

Utilizing Performance Reports

Next, we navigate to the "Performance Reports" section. MySQL Workbench offers a variety of pre-built reports that focus on key aspects of database performance. We open the "Top Queries" report to identify which SQL statements are consuming the most resources. We then review the "InnoDB Buffer Pool Efficiency" report, which indicates how effectively data is being cached. Additionally, you examine reports on "Slow Queries" and "Index Usage," which provide insights into possible areas for optimization.

Analyzing Query Performance with EXPLAIN

We also use MySQL Workbench's built-in EXPLAIN feature to analyze query execution plans. We run sample queries directly within the Workbench SQL Editor, and then click on the "Explain" button to generate a visual representation of the query plan. This output details how the MySQL optimizer processes the query, showing which indexes are used and where full table scans occur.

Analyzing and Interpreting Metrics

Interpreting Key Metrics

Once you have gathered performance metrics, you focus on interpreting the data. For instance, you examine CPU and memory graphs to see if there are any periods of sustained high usage, which might indicate the need for configuration adjustments such as increasing the InnoDB buffer pool size or optimizing query structures. Similarly, slow query reports point out queries that take longer than expected to execute. We correlate these findings with the EXPLAIN plans to decide on the best course of action for tuning those queries.

Setting up Alerts and Baselines

For ongoing monitoring, you can set up alerts in MySQL Workbench or integrate with external monitoring tools. Establishing baseline performance metrics is critical so that you can compare future performance after applying tuning adjustments. We record key metrics such as average query response time, CPU usage, and memory consumption. These baselines become reference points to measure the impact of any changes you make in the future.

Advanced Features and Customization

Custom Dashboards

MySQL Workbench also allows you to create custom dashboards that display the metrics most relevant to our GitforGits application. We can design a dashboard that focuses on performance-critical metrics such as query throughput, disk I/O rates, and replication lag (if applicable). This customization ensures that the monitoring environment is tailored to our specific needs and provides immediate visual feedback on system health.

Step 11: Integrating External Monitoring Tools

In addition to MySQL Workbench, you may choose to integrate external monitoring solutions like Prometheus or Grafana for more advanced analytics and long-term tracking. While MySQL Workbench provides a robust set of tools for real-time monitoring and analysis, external platforms can store historical data and trigger alerts based on predefined thresholds. We configure these tools to pull metrics from our MySQL instance and display them in customizable dashboards.

Analyze and Improve Queries

First, we will take a look at the key metrics that show how well the queries are performing. We will check the slow query log, look at how long queries are taking to execute, and review throughput data from our performance reports. These metrics help us figure out which queries are taking longer than expected and using up too many resources. We will go over how high CPU usage, long-running queries, and a lot of disk I/O are often signs of inefficient SQL. By looking at these metrics and the queries' execution plans, we can find the areas that need optimization.

Using EXPLAIN for Query Analysis

Running EXPLAIN

One of the most powerful tools at our disposal is the EXPLAIN statement. We log into MySQL Workbench and execute the EXPLAIN command on a query that has been flagged as slow. For example, you run:

```
EXPLAIN SELECT orders.order_id, customers.name,
orders.total_amount
FROM orders
JOIN customers ON orders.customer_id = customers.customer_id
WHERE orders.order_date >= '2024-01-01';
```

This command returns a detailed execution plan that shows how MySQL processes the query. We examine elements such as the order in which tables are accessed, which indexes are used, and whether any full table scans occur.

Interpreting Execution Plan

We discuss how to interpret key columns in the EXPLAIN output, such as:

- **id:** The sequence of execution.
- **select_type:** Whether the query is simple or a subquery.
- **table:** Which table is being accessed.
- **type:** The join type, where values like "ALL" indicate a full table scan.
- **possible_keys:** Indexes that could be used.
- **key:** The actual index used.
- **rows:** An estimate of the number of rows scanned.
- **Extra:** Additional details, such as "Using where" or "Using temporary."

These elements help you identify whether an index is missing or if the query is structured inefficiently.

Refining Query Structure and Indexing

Rewriting Queries

After analyzing the execution plan, we consider rewriting the query to improve its performance. For example, if our original query is causing a full table scan due to a non-indexed column in the WHERE clause, we might rewrite it to take advantage of an index. Suppose we discover that the **order_date** column is not indexed. We then proceed to add an index:

```
ALTER TABLE orders ADD INDEX idx_order_date (order_date);
```

After adding the index, we run the EXPLAIN command again to confirm that the query now uses the new index.

Optimizing Joins and Subqueries

We also examine join conditions and subqueries. In cases where a subquery is causing performance issues, we explore replacing it with a JOIN or a Common Table Expression (CTE). For example, if you have a query with a subquery that fetches customer details, you might restructure it as a join:

```
-- Original query with subquery
SELECT o.order_id,
       (SELECT name FROM customers WHERE customer_id =
o.customer_id) AS customer_name,
       o.total_amount
FROM orders o;
-- Optimized query using JOIN
SELECT o.order_id, c.name AS customer_name, o.total_amount
FROM orders o
JOIN customers c ON o.customer_id = c.customer_id;
```

We then use EXPLAIN on the new query to ensure it runs more efficiently.

Applying Index Optimization

We learned that indexes are needed for speeding up query execution. However, excessive or poorly designed indexes can also harm performance by increasing the overhead on write operations. We review the indexes on our key tables using:

```
SHOW INDEX FROM orders;
```

After analyzing the output, we decide to adjust the indexes based on our query patterns. For instance, if we notice that multiple queries filter on both **customer_id** and **order_date**, we create a composite index:

```
ALTER TABLE orders DROP INDEX idx_order_date;
ALTER TABLE orders ADD INDEX idx_customer_date (customer_id,
order_date);
```

This composite index reduces the number of rows scanned and speeds up queries that join orders with customers or filter by date.

Through the process of analyzing and improving queries, we learned how to identify performance bottlenecks by using EXPLAIN and performance metrics. We optimized our SQL statements by rewriting queries, adding appropriate indexes, and restructuring joins and subqueries. These enhancements directly improved query execution times and reduced resource consumption.

Design Effective Indexes

Role of Indexes

Indexes act like a roadmap for the database engine, allowing it to quickly locate and retrieve rows without scanning the entire table. We recognize that, while indexes can dramatically improve read performance, they also come with trade-offs. Each index consumes additional disk space and can slow down write operations due to extra maintenance overhead. Our goal is to strike a balance by creating indexes that cover our most frequently executed queries while avoiding unnecessary duplication.

Types of Indexes

Single-Column Indexes

We start with single-column indexes, which are created on individual columns that are frequently used in WHERE clauses or as join keys. For example, if our orders table is often queried by order_date, we create an index like this:

```
ALTER TABLE orders ADD INDEX idx_order_date (order_date);
```

This index enables the database engine to quickly filter rows based on the order date, reducing the need for a full table scan.

Composite Indexes

Sometimes, queries filter on multiple columns simultaneously. In these cases, composite indexes (or multi-column indexes) are highly effective. For instance, if our queries often involve filtering by both customer_id and order_date, we design a composite index:

```
ALTER TABLE orders ADD INDEX idx_customer_order (customer_id,
order_date);
```

We learn that the order of columns in a composite index is important; the index is most effective when the query conditions match the leftmost prefix of the index. We must consider our query patterns carefully to decide the correct order of columns.

Unique Indexes

Unique indexes enforce data uniqueness and also improve query performance by providing a fast lookup. When dealing with columns that must contain unique values, such as email addresses in a customers table, we create a unique index:

```
ALTER TABLE customers ADD UNIQUE INDEX idx_email (email);
```

This ensures both data integrity and efficient retrieval.

Create and Adjust Indexes

We begin by analyzing our query logs and performance metrics to identify which columns are frequently used in WHERE clauses, JOIN conditions, and ORDER BY clauses. This helps to determine the most beneficial indexes to create. The MySQL Workbench and EXPLAIN helps to pinpoint queries that suffer from slow performance.

Creating Indexes

Once we have identified candidate columns, we create indexes using the ALTER TABLE command. For example, if our products table is often queried by category and price range, we may create:

```
ALTER TABLE products ADD INDEX idx_category_price (category,
price);
```

This composite index allows for efficient retrieval of products within a specific category and price range.

Evaluating Index Effectiveness

After creating indexes, we use the EXPLAIN command to see how queries make use of them. For instance:

```
EXPLAIN SELECT * FROM orders WHERE customer_id = 101 AND
order_date >= '2024-01-01';
```

By reviewing the execution plan, we confirm that the appropriate indexes are being used. If the plan shows a full table scan instead of an index lookup, we revisit our index design or adjust our query to better match the index.

Adjusting and Removing Redundant Indexes

We also periodically review existing indexes to ensure they are still beneficial. Over time, as query patterns change or new indexes are added, some indexes might become redundant. We use:

```
SHOW INDEX FROM orders;
```

to review the current indexes and determine if any can be consolidated or removed. Eliminating unnecessary indexes helps reduce disk space usage and speeds up write operations.

Testing Under Load

Finally, we test our optimized queries under realistic workloads using tools like sysbench. By simulating high-concurrency scenarios, we verify that our indexes improve query performance and that the overhead of maintaining them does not adversely impact overall system performance.

The optimized indexes help our system retrieve data quickly, reducing query execution times and improving the app's overall responsiveness. Our development docs include details on index configurations and rationale, so our team knows the indexing strategy and can use it for similar projects.

Tune Buffers and Caches

We begin by exploring the critical memory settings that directly impact performance. The **InnoDB Buffer Pool** is one of the most important components, as it caches data and indexes for InnoDB tables. A larger buffer pool can significantly reduce disk reads and improve query performance. Additionally, parameters such as **query cache** (if enabled), **sort_buffer_size**, and **join_buffer_size** also play vital roles in managing temporary data during query execution. We review the current settings and compare them with best practices for our workload, ensuring that our system uses available memory efficiently.

Adjusting InnoDB Buffer Pool

Evaluate Current Buffer Pool Usage

We start by checking the current InnoDB buffer pool size and its hit ratio. By executing a query like:

```
SHOW GLOBAL STATUS LIKE 'Innodb_buffer_pool_%';
```

we can review metrics such as **`Innodb_buffer_pool_read_requests`** and **`Innodb_buffer_pool_reads`**. A high hit ratio indicates that most data requests are served from memory rather than disk, which is ideal. If the hit ratio is low, it might be necessary to increase the buffer pool size.

Modify Buffer Pool Size

We open the MySQL configuration file and adjust the InnoDB buffer pool size. For example, if our server has 16GB of RAM and is dedicated to MySQL, we might set:

```
[mysqld]
innodb_buffer_pool_size = 10G
```

This configuration allocates a significant portion of memory for caching, which helps minimize disk I/O. After making the change, we restart MySQL to apply the new settings:

```
sudo systemctl restart mysql
```

Validate Changes

Post-restart, we check the status again to confirm the buffer pool is operating as expected. We monitor the hit ratio over time using:

```
SHOW GLOBAL STATUS LIKE 'Innodb_buffer_pool_read%';
```

This helps us ensure that our modifications are improving performance.

Tuning Additional Memory Buffers

Adjusting Sort and Join Buffers

Next, we fine-tune memory settings related to query processing. Parameters like **sort_buffer_size** and **join_buffer_size** determine the amount of memory allocated for sorting operations and join processing, respectively. In our configuration file, we adjust these parameters based on our query workload. For example:

```
[mysqld]
```

```
sort_buffer_size = 2M
join_buffer_size = 4M
```

These settings help optimize operations that involve sorting or joining large datasets. We test the impact by running complex queries and observing execution times using the EXPLAIN command.

Configuring Query Cache

Although query cache is disabled by default in many modern MySQL installations due to potential contention issues, if our workload benefits from caching result sets, you can fine-tune it. We might set:

```
query_cache_size = 64M
query_cache_type = 1
```

We evaluate whether enabling query cache improves performance by testing frequently executed, read-heavy queries. If contention is observed, we consider keeping it disabled to avoid potential slowdowns.

With our buffers and caches finely tuned, we integrate these optimizations into our GitforGits application. The improved memory settings ensure that frequently accessed data is readily available, reducing disk I/O and speeding up query processing.

Summary

Overall, using MySQL Workbench and other monitoring tools helped us learn more about query performance and system tuning. We looked at important metrics like CPU usage, memory allocation, and disk I/O, and we learned how to use these to find places where performance is slowing down. We looked at query execution plans with the EXPLAIN command. This helped us find operations that were not using resources efficiently so we could change our queries to fix them. We were able to make useful indexes by finding the right balance between single-column and composite indexes to get the best data retrieval while avoiding extra work.

We also worked on fine-tuning the memory settings by changing the sizes of the InnoDB buffer pool, sort buffer, and join buffer. This made sure that frequently accessed data was always in memory and cut down on disk I/O. We confirmed that these changes made the system much more efficient and sped up response times to queries through iterative testing and benchmarking. We took an active role in keeping performance high by incorporating real-time monitoring and creating custom dashboards. We were also able to fine-tune our database environment with these hands-on activities, which made sure that our GitforGits application ran smoothly even when it had a lot of work to do. Overall, we learned useful skills in query optimization and system tuning that are necessary to keep a production MySQL environment that works well and can grow as needed.

Chapter 8: Master Data Management and Routine Maintenance

Overview

This chapter will teach you how to manage our data and do regular maintenance on our MySQL environment to keep it strong, scalable, and ready for future growth. Using methods like normalization, strategic denormalization, and horizontal partitioning, you will lear n to change our current schema to handle growing amounts of data while keeping the integrity of the data. We will learn useful ways to divide up big tables so that data can be retrieved faster and maintenance is easier.

We will also take strict steps to protect the integrity of the data by using constraints, triggers, and check conditions. We will also learn effective ways to optimize storage, such as how to compress data, fine-tune buffer pools, and change data types to lower disk I/O and latency. We will do hands-on activities and realistic situations throughout the chapter that show you how to keep an eye on, maintain, and keep making our database run better. By the end of this chapter, you can manage large-scale data efficiently and maintain a high-performing MySQL environment.

Reinvent Scalable Schema

The more our app grows, the more important it is to change the schema so that it can support more data in the future, as well as make it easy to search, integrate smoothly, and handle transactions. To do this, we need to find ways to organize, split, and combine data as needed, while keeping the relationships between entities consistent and making sure the system is ready for new needs.

Assessing Existing Schema

Evaluating Current Structure

We start by taking a close look at our current schema. We review the tables, relationships, and indexes that have been established so far. By analyzing query performance metrics and system usage patterns, we identify areas where the schema may be limiting our scalability. For instance, some tables might have redundant data or lack proper indexing, while others may be too normalized or overly denormalized for the current workload. We use tools such as MySQL Workbench to generate schema diagrams and assess table designs, focusing on key aspects like primary keys, foreign keys, and normalization levels.

Identifying Bottlenecks and Growth Areas

We gather insights from historical data usage and performance logs to pinpoint bottlenecks. Areas that experience high read or write contention, such as the orders or inventory tables, are flagged for potential redesign. We consider whether certain tables would benefit from horizontal partitioning or sharding to distribute load. It helps us to determine which parts of the schema require reinvention to support both current operations and anticipated growth.

Reinventing Schema

Draft New Schema Design

We begin by drafting a new schema design using diagramming tools like MySQL Workbench. This visual representation allows us to map out the relationships and data flow between tables, ensuring that the design meets scalability and integrity requirements. We document our design decisions, including the rationale for partitioning, the balance of normalization, and any anticipated trade-offs.

Create Test Tables and Migrate Data

Once the design is finalized, we create test tables in a development environment. We use SQL scripts to generate the new schema structure, including any partitions or modified columns:

```
CREATE TABLE orders_new (
    order_id INT AUTO_INCREMENT PRIMARY KEY,
    customer_id INT NOT NULL,
    order_date DATE NOT NULL,
    total_amount DECIMAL(10,2) NOT NULL,
    INDEX idx_order_date (order_date)
) ENGINE=InnoDB
PARTITION BY RANGE (YEAR(order_date)) (
    PARTITION p2020 VALUES LESS THAN (2021),
    PARTITION p2021 VALUES LESS THAN (2022),
    PARTITION p2022 VALUES LESS THAN (2023),
    PARTITION p2023 VALUES LESS THAN (2024)
);
```

We then migrate a subset of data from the existing orders table into the new structure. Using tools like **`mysqldump`** and **`LOAD DATA INFILE`**, we transfer data and validate that all records conform to the new schema's constraints.

Validate and Benchmark New Schema

After migrating data, we run a series of tests to compare performance between the old and new schemas. We execute common queries, such as those involving filtering by order date or joining with customer data, and use the EXPLAIN plan to analyze execution. We benchmark response times and resource usage, ensuring that the new schema delivers the expected performance improvements.

Iterate and Refine

Based on our testing, we refine the schema design as needed. This may involve adjusting partition boundaries, adding or modifying indexes, or fine-tuning data types to reduce storage overhead. We continue to iterate on the design until the new schema meets our performance and scalability objectives while maintaining robust data integrity.

Implementing Schema Changes in Production

Plan Rollout

Once satisfied with the test environment, we plan a gradual rollout for the production environment. We schedule maintenance windows, prepare backup strategies, and coordinate with stakeholders to ensure minimal disruption. Our rollout plan includes a comprehensive backup of the existing database, followed by a phased migration of schema changes.

Monitor and Adjust

After deployment, we continuously monitor the performance of the new schema using MySQL Workbench and other monitoring tools. We review key metrics such as query response times, disk I/O, and CPU usage to confirm that the production workload is handled efficiently. If any issues arise, we are prepared to make adjustments or rollback to the previous schema until the problems are resolved.

This all-inclusive approach let us tackle current performance issues and get our database ready for more work and changing business needs. Our process of designing, testing, and improving the schema has given us the skills we need to handle big data environments. This ensures that our app stays responsive, efficient, and able to grow over time.

Implement Table Partitioning

Overview

We will now move beyond small-scale partitioning and try to explore the practical techniques for splitting extensive datasets into manageable segments. This will help us to aim to reduce query response times, optimize disk I/O, and streamline administrative operations like backups and archiving. It will let us maintain high performance as our data grows.

So here, we begin by understanding that table partitioning divides a large table into smaller, more manageable pieces while still treating the data as a single logical table. This division is based on a specified key, such as a date or region, which helps in limiting the amount of data scanned during queries. We are aware that partitioning can lead to significant performance improvements because the query optimizer can skip irrelevant partitions entirely. Moreover, maintenance tasks such as index rebuilding or purging outdated data become more efficient, as operations can be performed on individual partitions rather than the entire table.

Planning Partitioning Strategy

Identifying Partitioning Key

We carefully choose the partitioning key based on our query patterns. In our GitforGits application, we might consider partitioning the orders table by order date. This choice is based on the fact that many queries filter on order dates, and older partitions can be archived or purged without affecting recent data. We plan to partition data by year or quarter, which helps in handling high volumes of data over time.

Deciding Partitioning Method

We decide on the partitioning method that best suits our needs. MySQL supports various partitioning types, such as RANGE, LIST, HASH, and KEY. For our orders table, RANGE partitioning is ideal because it allows us to create partitions based on a continuous range of values, such as date intervals. We plan to create partitions for each year, which will let us quickly access recent data while isolating older records.

Implementing Table Partitioning

Creating a Partitioned Table

We start by designing the partitioned table for our orders data. Suppose our existing orders table has the following structure:

```
CREATE TABLE orders (
    order_id INT AUTO_INCREMENT PRIMARY KEY,
    customer_id INT NOT NULL,
    order_date DATE NOT NULL,
    total_amount DECIMAL(10,2) NOT NULL,
    status VARCHAR(50),
    INDEX idx_order_date (order_date)
) ENGINE=InnoDB;
```

We now convert this table into a partitioned table using RANGE partitioning based on the order_date. We drop the old table in our development environment or create a new one for testing. For example:

```
CREATE TABLE orders_partitioned (
    order_id INT AUTO_INCREMENT PRIMARY KEY,
    customer_id INT NOT NULL,
    order_date DATE NOT NULL,
    total_amount DECIMAL(10,2) NOT NULL,
    status VARCHAR(50),
    INDEX idx_order_date (order_date)
) ENGINE=InnoDB
PARTITION BY RANGE (YEAR(order_date)) (
    PARTITION p2020 VALUES LESS THAN (2021),
    PARTITION p2021 VALUES LESS THAN (2022),
    PARTITION p2022 VALUES LESS THAN (2023),
    PARTITION p2023 VALUES LESS THAN (2024),
    PARTITION p_future VALUES LESS THAN MAXVALUE
);
```

In the above sample program, we partition the orders table by year, creating separate partitions for orders in 2020, 2021, 2022, and 2023. Any orders with a year beyond 2023 will be stored in the **p_future** partition. This structure enables the database to scan only the relevant partition when a query filters on order_date, thereby improving performance.

Migrating Data into Partitioned Table

Next, we migrate data from the original orders table to our new partitioned table. We use an INSERT INTO ... SELECT statement to transfer data:

```
INSERT INTO orders_partitioned (order_id, customer_id,
order_date, total_amount, status)
SELECT order_id, customer_id, order_date, total_amount, status
FROM orders;
```

We verify that the data is correctly distributed across partitions by executing:

```
SELECT PARTITION, COUNT(*) AS rows_per_partition
FROM INFORMATION_SCHEMA.PARTITIONS
WHERE TABLE_SCHEMA = 'your_database' AND TABLE_NAME =
'orders_partitioned'
GROUP BY PARTITION;
```

This query shows the number of rows in each partition, confirming that our partitioning scheme is working as intended.

Testing Query Performance

We then test the performance improvements by running queries that filter on order_date. For instance:

```
EXPLAIN SELECT * FROM orders_partitioned WHERE order_date
BETWEEN '2022-01-01' AND '2022-12-31';
```

The EXPLAIN plan should indicate that only the partition corresponding to 2022 (p2022) is accessed. This reduced scan scope leads to faster query response times. We compare execution times of queries on the partitioned table versus the non-partitioned table and observe the performance gains.

Maintenance Benefits of Partitioning

Simplified Data Management

Partitioning not only improves query performance but also simplifies maintenance tasks. For example, if we need to purge data from previous years, we can drop an entire partition instead of deleting rows one by one. To remove data for 2020, we execute:

```
ALTER TABLE orders_partitioned DROP PARTITION p2020;
```

This operation is significantly faster than executing a DELETE query that scans and removes millions of rows.

Efficient Backups and Restores

We also note that partitioning can improve backup and restore operations. Since partitions are stored separately, we can back up or restore only the necessary partitions, reducing downtime and resource usage during these maintenance windows.

Managing Data Growth

As our GitforGits application grows, partitioning allows us to scale our database horizontally. We can add new partitions for future years without disrupting the existing schema. For example, to add a partition for 2024, we run:

```
ALTER TABLE orders_partitioned ADD PARTITION (
    PARTITION p2024 VALUES LESS THAN (2025)
);
```

This flexibility ensures that our schema adapts to increasing data volumes seamlessly.

Throughout this process, we adhere to best practices for table partitioning:

- Ensure that the chosen key (order_date in our case) is frequently used in queries to maximize performance gains.
- Regularly review the distribution of data across partitions to prevent any single partition from becoming a bottleneck.
- Design partitioning schemes that can easily accommodate additional data, such as by creating partitions for upcoming years.
- Maintain clear documentation on partitioning rules and maintenance procedures to help team members understand and manage the schema effectively.

The partitioning strategy successfully enhances the scalability of our database and ensures our system remains responsive as data volumes increase.

Enforce Data Integrity

We begin by understanding that data integrity encompasses several aspects: ensuring that the data entered into our database is valid, consistent, and adheres to predefined business rules. This reduces the risk of anomalies and maintain the reliability of our database. This process involves setting up constraints on tables, creating triggers to automate validations, and using check constraints to enforce specific conditions on the data.

Implementing Constraints

Primary and Foreign Keys

One of the first steps in enforcing data integrity is to ensure that our tables have proper primary and foreign keys. Primary keys uniquely identify each record, while foreign keys maintain the relationships between tables. For example, the **`orders`** table should reference the **`customers`** table. We implement these constraints as follows:

```
CREATE TABLE customers (
    customer_id INT AUTO_INCREMENT PRIMARY KEY,
    name VARCHAR(255) NOT NULL,
    email VARCHAR(255) UNIQUE,
    contact_number VARCHAR(20)
) ENGINE=InnoDB;
CREATE TABLE orders (
    order_id INT AUTO_INCREMENT PRIMARY KEY,
    customer_id INT NOT NULL,
    order_date DATE NOT NULL,
    total_amount DECIMAL(10,2) NOT NULL,
    FOREIGN KEY (customer_id) REFERENCES
customers(customer_id)
) ENGINE=InnoDB;
```

These constraints ensure that every order is associated with a valid customer, and that customer identifiers are unique and consistent.

Unique and Not Null Constraints

We further enforce data quality by adding unique and not null constraints on columns where applicable. For example, the email address in the **customers** table must be unique, and critical fields like **name** and **order_date** must always have valid values. This is implemented using the UNIQUE and NOT NULL keywords, as seen in the table definitions above. These constraints prevent duplicate entries and ensure that essential data is not missing.

Creating Triggers for Data Validation

Automating Business Logic

Triggers allow us to automatically enforce business rules whenever data is inserted, updated, or deleted. For our project, we can create a trigger to ensure that any new order has a valid total amount that is greater than zero. This helps prevent erroneous data from being entered into the system. Consider the following example:

```
DELIMITER $$
CREATE TRIGGER before_order_insert
```

```
BEFORE INSERT ON orders
FOR EACH ROW
BEGIN
    IF NEW.total_amount <= 0 THEN
        SIGNAL SQLSTATE '45000'
            SET MESSAGE_TEXT = 'Total amount must be greater than zero';
    END IF;
END$$
DELIMITER ;
```

This trigger checks the **total_amount** for each new order. If the amount is less than or equal to zero, it prevents the insertion and returns an error message. Similarly, you can create triggers to log changes or update related tables automatically, ensuring consistency across our data.

Enforcing Referential Integrity

Triggers can also be used to enforce referential integrity beyond simple foreign key constraints. For example, if our application requires that every order record should have an associated status entry in a related table, a trigger can verify this before the order is committed. By automating such validations, you ensure that our database remains consistent and adheres to the defined business logic.

Adding Check Constraints and Testing Data Integrity

While MySQL supports check constraints starting from version 8.0.16, they can be very effective in ensuring that data falls within acceptable ranges. For example, you might want to ensure that the **total_amount** in the orders table is within a realistic range:

```
ALTER TABLE orders
ADD CONSTRAINT chk_total_amount CHECK (total_amount > 0 AND total_amount < 10000);
```

This constraint automatically prevents any order with a **total_amount** outside the specified range from being inserted or updated. Similarly, you can add check constraints to validate formats, such as ensuring that the order date is not in the future.

Once constraints, triggers, and check conditions are in place, we test them to ensure they function as intended. We perform a series of insert, update, and delete operations to see if the system correctly rejects invalid data. For instance, we attempt to insert an order with a total amount of zero and verify that the trigger prevents the insertion:

```
INSERT INTO orders (customer_id, order_date, total_amount)
VALUES (1, '2024-04-01', 0);
```

If the trigger is working correctly, MySQL will return an error message indicating that the total amount must be greater than zero. We also test foreign key constraints by trying to insert an order with a non-existent customer_id, ensuring that the system maintains referential integrity. We can use the "Schema Inspector" to view the constraints on each table and the "SQL Editor" to run test queries.

Throughout this process, we adhered to best practices to maintain data integrity:

- Clearly document the rules and constraints that our data must adhere to.
- Implement primary, foreign, unique, and check constraints where applicable.
- Utilize triggers to enforce business logic automatically and ensure consistent data processing.
- Regularly test our integrity mechanisms with various scenarios to confirm they work as intended.
- Use monitoring tools and logging to audit changes and detect any integrity issues early.

This reinforcement has minimized errors and improved the reliability of our application, allowing us to maintain a high standard of data quality as the project scales.

Optimize Storage Management

We will now implement proven practices such as data compression, careful schema design, regular table maintenance, and hardware-level optimizations. Before making any changes, we start by evaluating our current storage usage. We use the following command to review table sizes, fragmentation, and free space:

```
SHOW TABLE STATUS FROM bookdepot;
```

This command provides insights into each table's data length, index length, and fragmentation.

Implementing Data Compression

Enabling InnoDB Compression

One of the most effective practices for reducing storage footprint is enabling InnoDB compression on large tables. For instance, if our **orders** table has grown considerably, we can alter it to use compressed row formats. First, we verify the current row format:

```
SHOW TABLE STATUS LIKE 'orders';
```

If it's not already compressed, we modify the table:

```
ALTER TABLE orders ENGINE=InnoDB, ROW_FORMAT=COMPRESSED,
KEY_BLOCK_SIZE=8;
```

This command converts the table to a compressed format using a key block size of 8KB. We then monitor the performance impact by checking the disk usage before and after the change using:

```
SELECT table_name, data_length, index_length
FROM information_schema.tables
WHERE table_schema = 'bookdepot' AND table_name = 'orders';
```

Adjusting Data Types

We revisit our schema to ensure that we are using efficient data types. For example, if a column defined as **TEXT** stores only short strings, we modify it to **VARCHAR(255)**, which uses less space:

```
ALTER TABLE products MODIFY COLUMN description VARCHAR(255);
```

This adjustment reduces the overall table size and improves index performance.

Configuring InnoDB Table

We enable the **innodb_file_per_table** setting to ensure that each InnoDB table is stored in its own file. This approach helps in managing and reclaiming disk space efficiently when tables are dropped or optimized. In our MySQL configuration file, we add:

```
[mysqld]
innodb_file_per_table = 1
```

After updating the configuration, we restart MySQL:

```
sudo systemctl restart mysql
```

This setting allows us to run the **OPTIMIZE TABLE** command more effectively on individual tables.

Regular Table Maintenance

Optimizing Tables

As data is inserted, updated, and deleted, tables can become fragmented. We then run the periodic maintenance task such as **OPTIMIZE TABLE** to defragment the data and reclaim unused space:

```
OPTIMIZE TABLE orders;
```

We schedule this command to run during off-peak hours using cron jobs or MySQL event scheduler. For instance, to run it nightly, we might create a script:

```
#!/bin/bash
mysql -u root -p'YourPassword' -e "OPTIMIZE TABLE orders;"
bookdepot
```

And add it to crontab:

```
0 3 * * * /path/to/optimize_orders.sh
```

Rebuilding Indexes

Index fragmentation can also degrade performance. We review indexes periodically with:

```
SHOW INDEX FROM orders;
```

If necessary, we drop and recreate indexes to ensure they are efficient:

```
ALTER TABLE orders DROP INDEX idx_order_date;
ALTER TABLE orders ADD INDEX idx_order_date (order_date);
```

This process minimizes index bloat and improves query response times.

Optimizing Disk I/O and File System

We ensure that our MySQL data directory is located on high-performance storage, such as SSDs, to reduce latency. In addition, using RAID configurations (e.g., RAID 10) can balance performance with redundancy. We work with our system administrator to verify that the underlying hardware is optimized for database workloads.

We also examine file system settings that affect disk performance. On Linux, adjusting the I/O scheduler to a "deadline" or "noop" scheduler for SSDs can improve performance. For example, we check the current scheduler with:

```
cat /sys/block/sda/queue/scheduler
```

And set it to "deadline" if beneficial:

```
echo deadline | sudo tee /sys/block/sda/queue/scheduler
```

These hardware-level tweaks complement our MySQL configuration changes.

Leveraging Caching and Buffer Pools

We revisit our InnoDB buffer pool settings to ensure that frequently accessed data remains in memory. The buffer pool is critical for reducing disk I/O. We assess its usage with:

```
SHOW GLOBAL STATUS LIKE 'Innodb_buffer_pool_%';
```

Based on our observations, we adjust the buffer pool size in our configuration file:

```
[mysqld]
innodb_buffer_pool_size = 10G
```

After making changes, we monitor the hit ratio to confirm that the majority of reads are served from memory rather than disk.

Another thing is that if query cache is applicable, we review its performance. In some environments, enabling a modest query cache can reduce repeated query processing:

```
query_cache_size = 64M
query_cache_type = 1
```

We evaluate its impact carefully, as query cache can sometimes create contention issues in write-heavy environments. Our adjustments are based on workload analysis and real-time monitoring. All these storage optimization techniques result in a more efficient database, with faster query response times and reduced disk I/O.

Summary

Overall, we restructured our database management strategy by completely overhauling the schema to support future growth and ensure data integrity. W e primarily looked at our current design, found any problems, and changed the way the tables were set up to find a good balance between normalization and selective denormalization. For better query performance and easier maintenance, horizontal partitioning was used to break up big tables into manageable chunks. We also made sure that the data was correct by setting strict constraints, triggers, and check conditions.

This way, business rules were always followed and the connections between tables stayed the same.

At the same time, we improved overall storage management by using data compression methods and changing the types of data to cut down on duplicates and boost disk I/O performance. We fine-tuned important memory settings, like the InnoDB buffer pool, to get the most out of caching. This cut latency even more and made query responses faster. Our plan included changing the settings for the file system and making sure that our hardware, like SSDs and RAID configurations, was strong enough to handle heavy workloads.

Through ongoing monitoring and planned maintenance, we kept track of all the changes we made and, based on performance metrics, made our configurations better over time. This thorough and proactive plan not only made the system more responsive overall, but it also set up our environment to handle more data without any problems.

Chapter 9: Leverage Advanced SQL and Transaction Control

Overview

In this chapter, you will explore advanced SQL techniques and transaction control strategies that will elevate our data management capabilities. We will begin by mastering Common Table Expressions (CTEs), learning not only how to simplify complex queries but also how to handle hierarchical data using recursive CTEs and correlated subqueries. We will then delve into window functions, which will enable you to perform sophisticated data analysis such as ranking, running totals, and comparing rows without the need for cumbersome subqueries.

We will also learn how to precisely manage transactions by learning how to use commit, rollback, and savepoint operations to make sure that data is always the same, even when mistakes happen. We will also balance isolation levels to optimize concurrency while preserving the integrity of our data, and you will explore strategies to resolve transaction conflicts and deadlocks. In each section, you'll find hands-on exercises that are meant to prepare you for real-life situations and give you the confidence to handle complex database operations. By the end of this chapter, you'll have a full set of advanced SQL and transaction management skills that will help our queries run faster and our ability to do analysis better.

Use Common Table Expressions (CTEs)

CTEs Overview

CTEs provide a way to break down complex queries into simpler, more manageable parts. They can be especially useful when working with hierarchical or recursive data, and they enhance query clarity by allowing you to name intermediate results. In its simplest form, a CTE is defined using the WITH clause:

```
WITH recent_orders AS (
    SELECT order_id, customer_id, order_date, total_amount
    FROM orders
    WHERE order_date >= '2024-01-01'
)
SELECT * FROM recent_orders;
```

In the above sample program, the CTE **recent_orders** temporarily store orders from 2024, which is then used by the main query to display the results. This approach makes the query easier to understand and maintain compared to using a nested subquery.

Recursive CTEs

Recursive CTEs extend the power of CTEs by allowing you to work with hierarchical or recursive data structures. They consist of two parts: an anchor member and a recursive member. The anchor member defines the base result, and the recursive member repeatedly references the CTE to build on the anchor's results.

Imagine our GitforGits application maintains a category hierarchy for books. Each category might have a parent category, forming a tree structure. We can use a recursive CTE to traverse this hierarchy. Consider a table **categories** with columns **category_id**, **category_name**, and **parent_id**:

```
CREATE TABLE categories (
    category_id INT AUTO_INCREMENT PRIMARY KEY,
    category_name VARCHAR(255) NOT NULL,
    parent_id INT DEFAULT NULL,
    FOREIGN KEY (parent_id) REFERENCES categories(category_id)
);
```

To retrieve the full hierarchy starting from a top-level category, we write:

```
WITH RECURSIVE category_tree AS (
    -- Anchor member: select the root category
    SELECT category_id, category_name, parent_id, 0 AS level
    FROM categories
    WHERE parent_id IS NULL
    UNION ALL
    -- Recursive member: select child categories
    SELECT c.category_id, c.category_name, c.parent_id,
ct.level + 1 AS level
    FROM categories c
    INNER JOIN category_tree ct ON c.parent_id =
ct.category_id
)
SELECT * FROM category_tree
ORDER BY level, category_id;
```

This recursive CTE, **category_tree**, starts with the root categories (where **parent_id** is NULL) and then repeatedly joins with the **categories** table to include child categories, incrementing the **level** at each step. The result is a hierarchical list of categories that clearly shows the relationship and depth of each category.

Correlated Subqueries within CTEs

CTEs can also incorporate correlated subqueries to refine the data further. A correlated subquery is one that references columns from the outer query, and when used within a CTE, it allows for dynamic filtering based on computed values. For instance, if we want to enrich our orders data with aggregated information, such as the total number of orders for each customer, we can incorporate a correlated subquery in our CTE.

Suppose we want to list recent orders along with the total order count for each customer. We can define a CTE that computes the order count and then join it with our orders:

```
WITH customer_order_summary AS (
    SELECT customer_id, COUNT(*) AS order_count
    FROM orders
    GROUP BY customer_id
),
recent_orders AS (
    SELECT o.order_id, o.customer_id, o.order_date,
o.total_amount,
           (SELECT cos.order_count
            FROM customer_order_summary cos
            WHERE cos.customer_id = o.customer_id) AS
customer_order_count
    FROM orders o
    WHERE o.order_date >= '2024-01-01'
)
SELECT * FROM recent_orders;
```

In the above sample program, the **customer_order_summary** CTE computes the total number of orders per customer. Then, the **recent_orders** CTE selects orders from 2024 and uses a correlated subquery to fetch the order count for each customer from the summary CTE. This integration of correlated subqueries within CTEs helps us create enriched, context-aware datasets.

Sample Program: Combining CTEs for Book Orders Reporting

Imagine you need to generate a report for the GitforGits Book Depot that includes recent orders along with customer order history and category hierarchies. We can combine basic, recursive, and correlated CTEs to achieve this.

We start with a CTE that filters recent orders.

```
WITH recent_orders AS (
    SELECT order_id, customer_id, order_date, total_amount
    FROM orders
    WHERE order_date >= '2024-01-01'
),
```

Next, we add a CTE that calculates total orders per customer.

```
customer_order_summary AS (
    SELECT customer_id, COUNT(*) AS total_orders
    FROM orders
    GROUP BY customer_id
),
```

Finally, we combine these CTEs to display recent orders enriched with customer history.

```
enriched_recent_orders AS (
    SELECT r.order_id, r.customer_id, r.order_date,
r.total_amount,
        (SELECT total_orders
         FROM customer_order_summary
         WHERE customer_id = r.customer_id) AS
customer_total_orders
    FROM recent_orders r
)
SELECT * FROM enriched_recent_orders;
```

Sample Program: Navigating Category Hierarchies

For another practical application, we revisit the recursive CTE example to traverse category hierarchies. Suppose we need to display the entire category tree for our book inventory, highlighting each category's depth and structure. We can use the recursive CTE we demonstrated earlier:

```
WITH RECURSIVE category_tree AS (
    SELECT category_id, category_name, parent_id, 0 AS level
    FROM categories
    WHERE parent_id IS NULL
    UNION ALL
    SELECT c.category_id, c.category_name, c.parent_id,
ct.level + 1 AS level
    FROM categories c
    INNER JOIN category_tree ct ON c.parent_id =
ct.category_id
)
SELECT * FROM category_tree
ORDER BY level, category_id;
```

This query provides a complete view of the category hierarchy, which can be integrated into our reporting system to display book categories in an organized, hierarchical manner.

These CTE techniques let us create advanced SQL queries that are both efficient and easy to maintain. When we used these methods in our GitforGits application, we really improved how well we could generate insightful reports and handle complex data relationships. This gave us powerful tools to manage our evolving data needs.

Explore Window Functions

Window Functions Overview

Window functions let you perform calculations across sets of rows related to the current row, which can be incredibly useful for tasks like ranking, running totals, moving averages, and comparing rows within partitions of data. Window functions operate over a “window” of rows that are defined by the OVER clause. Unlike regular aggregate functions, they do not collapse rows into a single output; instead, they allow you to retain the original row data while computing additional insights. For example, if you need to rank orders by total amount or calculate a running total of sales, window functions provide a concise and efficient way to do so.

We will explore several important window functions:

- **ROW_NUMBER()** assigns a unique sequential number to rows within a partition.
- **RANK()** and **DENSE_RANK()** assign ranking values to rows, with differences in handling ties.
- **LAG()** and **LEAD()** allow you to access data from previous or subsequent rows within the same partition.
- **SUM() OVER (...)** computes cumulative totals, while similar functions can calculate averages, counts, and more.

Implementing Window Functions

Ranking Orders by Total Amount

Imagine we need to rank customer orders by total amount in descending order. We can use the ROW_NUMBER() function to assign a rank to each order within the overall dataset:

```
SELECT
    order_id,
    customer_id,
    total_amount,
    ROW_NUMBER() OVER (ORDER BY total_amount DESC) AS
order_rank
FROM orders;
```

In this query, each order receives a unique rank based on its total_amount. If you want to account for ties in order amounts, you might use RANK() instead:

```
SELECT
    order_id,
    customer_id,
    total_amount,
    RANK() OVER (ORDER BY total_amount DESC) AS order_rank
FROM orders;
```

This function gives the same rank to orders with identical total amounts, with subsequent ranks skipping accordingly.

Calculating Running Totals

Next, consider calculating a running total of sales over a period. This is useful for tracking cumulative sales trends:

```
SELECT
    order_date,
    total_amount,
    SUM(total_amount) OVER (ORDER BY order_date ROWS BETWEEN
UNBOUNDED PRECEDING AND CURRENT ROW) AS running_total
FROM orders
WHERE order_date >= '2024-01-01';
```

In the above, the SUM() function operates as a window function, adding up the total_amount values from the beginning of the partition (or dataset) up to the current row. This running total gives you insight into how sales accumulate over time.

Analyzing Trends with LAG() and LEAD()

For more nuanced analysis, window functions like LAG() and LEAD() let you compare values across rows. Suppose you want to see the previous day's total_amount for each order to analyze day-to-day changes:

```
SELECT
    order_date,
    total_amount,
    LAG(total_amount, 1) OVER (ORDER BY order_date) AS
previous_total
FROM orders
WHERE order_date >= '2024-01-01';
```

Likewise, LEAD() allows you to peek at the following row:

```
SELECT
    order_date,
```

```
    total_amount,
    LEAD(total_amount, 1) OVER (ORDER BY order_date) AS
next_total
FROM orders
WHERE order_date >= '2024-01-01';
```

These functions are extremely useful for calculating differences, growth rates, or for creating alerts when a significant change in values is detected.

Partitioning Data for Group-Specific Analysis

Often, it's beneficial to analyze data within subgroups. For instance, you may want to calculate the cumulative sales for each customer separately. By partitioning the data by customer_id, window functions can compute values for each group independently:

```
SELECT
    customer_id,
    order_date,
    total_amount,
    SUM(total_amount) OVER (PARTITION BY customer_id ORDER BY
order_date) AS customer_running_total
FROM orders
WHERE order_date >= '2024-01-01';
```

This query resets the running total for each customer, providing a clear picture of individual purchasing behavior over time.

By going through all these window functions, we learned how to rank rows, calculate running totals, and compare data across rows using functions like ROW_NUMBER(), RANK(), LAG(), and LEAD(). Moreover, partitioning data within window functions allowed us to tailor our analysis to specific groups, such as individual customers. This hands-on approach simplified our SQL queries and also improved performance with deeper insights into our business data.

Manage Transactions

Transactions provide atomicity, consistency, isolation, and durability (ACID properties) in database operations. We learn that these properties guarantee that our operations are processed reliably, even when multiple users or applications interact with the database concurrently. In our

GitforGits application, transactions are crucial when performing tasks like order processing, where multiple related operations must succeed together. If any part of the transaction fails, we can use rollback operations to revert the changes, ensuring that our database remains in a consistent state.

Practical Transaction Management

Starting a Transaction

To begin, we use the START TRANSACTION command to initiate a new transaction. For example, when processing a new order, we might insert records into several tables:

```
START TRANSACTION;
INSERT INTO orders (customer_id, order_date, total_amount)
VALUES (101, NOW(), 59.99);
INSERT INTO order_items (order_id, product_id, quantity,
price)
VALUES (LAST_INSERT_ID(), 205, 2, 29.99);
```

By starting a transaction, we ensure that these related operations are treated as a single unit.

Using Savepoints

Within a long transaction, we might want to create savepoints to allow partial rollbacks. For instance, if our order processing involves several steps, we can set a savepoint after inserting the order record:

```
SAVEPOINT order_created;
```

After setting the savepoint, we continue with additional operations, such as updating inventory:

```
UPDATE inventory
SET stock = stock - 2
WHERE product_id = 205;
```

If an error occurs in the subsequent steps, we can roll back to the savepoint rather than canceling the entire transaction.

Committing Transaction

Once all operations in the transaction are successfully executed, we use the COMMIT command to permanently save the changes:

```
COMMIT;
```

With this, all the modifications, from inserting orders to updating inventory, are applied atomically, and the database remains consistent.

Handling Errors with Rollback

In real-world scenarios, errors might occur during the transaction. If an error is detected, we use the ROLLBACK command to undo changes. For example, if updating inventory fails due to insufficient stock, we can revert to the savepoint:

```
ROLLBACK TO SAVEPOINT order_created;
```

If the error is critical and affects the entire transaction, we perform a full rollback:

```
ROLLBACK;
```

This command reverts all operations performed in the current transaction, ensuring that no partial updates corrupt the data.

Sample Program: Order Processing Workflow

Let us think of a situation wherein if a customer places an order, multiple operations need to be executed: inserting the order record, adding each item to the order_items table, and updating the inventory accordingly. We wrap these operations in a transaction to ensure data consistency.

First, we begin by initiating the transaction to ensure that all subsequent operations are treated as a single unit.

```
START TRANSACTION;
```

We then insert the main order record.

```
INSERT INTO orders (customer_id, order_date, total_amount)
VALUES (101, NOW(), 59.99);
```

Immediately after inserting the order, we set a savepoint.

```
SAVEPOINT order_created;
```

Next, we insert each order item, referencing the order record using LAST_INSERT_ID().

```
INSERT INTO order_items (order_id, product_id, quantity,
price)
```

```
VALUES (LAST_INSERT_ID(), 205, 2, 29.99);
```

We then update the inventory, reducing stock levels based on the order.

```
UPDATE inventory
SET stock = stock - 2
WHERE product_id = 205;
```

Now suppose the inventory update fails due to insufficient stock. We then rollback to the savepoint, preserving the order record while canceling the inventory update.

```
ROLLBACK TO SAVEPOINT order_created;
```

After handling the error (e.g., notifying the user about insufficient stock), we either commit the transaction if all operations are correct or perform a full rollback if critical errors persist.

```
COMMIT;
```

or

```
ROLLBACK;
```

This workflow ensures that partial data is not committed in the event of an error and that our database remains in a consistent state throughout the order processing lifecycle. By handling errors gracefully with savepoints and rollbacks, we prevented data corruption and maintained the reliability of our database.

Balance Isolation Levels

We're going to try to tackle the challenges of concurrency by taking a look at isolation levels in MySQL 9. We know that our GitforGits application has a lot of concurrent operations, so we are facing issues like dirty reads, non-repeatable reads, and phantom reads, which can mess up the data. We're going to bring up the idea of isolation levels and show you how to set these up to get the best concurrency while making sure the data stays consistent and reliable.

Understanding Isolation Levels

Isolation levels define the degree to which the operations in one transaction are isolated from those in other concurrent transactions. MySQL supports several isolation levels:

- **READ UNCOMMITTED:** The lowest level, where transactions can see uncommitted changes made by others. This level offers maximum concurrency but risks dirty reads.

- **READ COMMITTED:** Only committed data is visible, which prevents dirty reads. However, non-repeatable reads and phantom reads might occur.
- **REPEATABLE READ:** The default level in MySQL, which ensures that multiple reads within the same transaction are consistent. Although it prevents non-repeatable reads, phantom reads may still be possible.
- **SERIALIZABLE:** The highest level of isolation, ensuring complete isolation by locking the entire dataset. While this prevents all concurrency issues, it can significantly reduce performance due to high locking overhead.

We will assess the trade-offs between these levels to decide which one best suits our workload, ensuring that our system can handle concurrent operations without compromising data integrity.

Configuring Isolation Levels

Checking Current Isolation Level

We start by checking the current isolation level for our MySQL instance. We log into the MySQL shell and run:

```
SHOW VARIABLES LIKE 'tx_isolation';
```

or, in more recent versions:

```
SHOW VARIABLES LIKE 'transaction_isolation';
```

This command tells us the default isolation level (typically REPEATABLE READ in MySQL 9). Understanding the current setting helps us plan adjustments based on our concurrency needs.

Adjusting Isolation Levels at Session or Global Level

We can modify the isolation level either for a specific session or globally. To set the isolation level for the current session, we use:

```
SET SESSION transaction_isolation = 'READ COMMITTED';
```

This change applies only to the session in which it is set, making it useful for testing how different isolation levels affect concurrent transactions without altering the entire system.

For a global change, which affects all new sessions, we run:

```
SET GLOBAL transaction_isolation = 'READ COMMITTED';
```

This command updates the default isolation level for all subsequent connections. We consider adjusting the global setting if our tests indicate that a lower isolation level (like READ

COMMITTED) improves concurrency without risking data integrity issues.

Testing Concurrency Scenarios

With isolation levels adjusted, we test their impact on concurrent operations. We simulate multiple transactions that interact with the same data. For example, we start two sessions:

- Session 1:

```
SET SESSION transaction_isolation = 'REPEATABLE READ';
START TRANSACTION;
SELECT * FROM orders WHERE order_id = 101;
```

- Session 2:

```
SET SESSION transaction_isolation = 'REPEATABLE READ';
START TRANSACTION;
UPDATE orders SET total_amount = total_amount + 10 WHERE
order_id = 101;
COMMIT;
```

In Session 1, we run the same SELECT query again after Session 2 commits its update:

```
SELECT * FROM orders WHERE order_id = 101;
```

We observe whether Session 1 sees the updated value. Under REPEATABLE READ, it might not, due to the isolation properties, whereas under READ COMMITTED, it should reflect the latest committed data. These tests help us evaluate the balance between data consistency and concurrency.

Analyzing Trade-Offs

We will go over what the different levels mean as below:

- **READ UNCOMMITTED** offers the highest concurrency but risks dirty reads, which could lead to inconsistent reporting or data corruption.
- **READ COMMITTED** prevents dirty reads and offers a good balance between performance and consistency, though it may allow non-repeatable reads.
- **REPEATABLE READ** ensures that once data is read, it remains consistent within the transaction. This level is ideal for most operations in our project but can sometimes introduce locking delays in high-concurrency situations.

- **SERIALIZABLE** guarantees complete isolation, but its strict locking can severely limit performance in a busy environment.

In our application, we evaluate whether REPEATABLE READ provides sufficient consistency or if switching to READ COMMITTED would yield better performance in high-concurrency scenarios without risking data integrity.

Fine-Tuning Isolation Levels in Specific Transactions

We also consider applying different isolation levels to specific transactions based on their criticality. For instance, when processing a customer order, data consistency is paramount. In such cases, we maintain a higher isolation level, such as REPEATABLE READ. For reporting queries that aggregate data and do not require absolute consistency, we might opt for READ COMMITTED to benefit from higher concurrency.

```
-- Critical transaction (order processing)
SET SESSION transaction_isolation = 'REPEATABLE READ';
START TRANSACTION;
-- execute critical operations
COMMIT;
-- Non-critical transaction (reporting)
SET SESSION transaction_isolation = 'READ COMMITTED';
START TRANSACTION;
-- execute reporting queries
COMMIT;
```

This flexible approach allows us to optimize performance where strict consistency is not necessary while preserving data integrity where it matters most.

By tweaking the isolation levels, we set things up so that important transactions kept their data integrity when REPEATABLE READ was enabled, while less sensitive operations gained from the extra concurrency offered by READ COMMITTED. This balanced approach cut down on lock contention and made the system overall quicker to respond. This made sure our database operations stayed efficient, even during the busiest times.

Resolve Transaction Conflicts

When there's a bunch of transactions competing for the same resources at once, it can lead to a deadlock, which is when two or more transactions are waiting for each other to release their locks.

This creates a cycle of dependency that stops all the processes.

Here's an example: Transaction A might lock Table X and ask for a lock on Table Y, while Transaction B might lock Table Y and be waiting for Table X to be free. In situations like this, neither transaction can proceed, and the database has to step in to resolve the deadlock.

We learned that deadlocks can have several causes, including:

- Multiple transactions updating the same rows in different orders.
- Coarse-grained locks that cover too many rows or tables, increasing the chance of conflicts.
- High system load and concurrent transactions increasing the likelihood of conflicting lock requests.

These above causes help us identify the points in our SQL code where conflicts are most likely to occur.

Identifying Deadlocks

MySQL automatically detects deadlocks and writes detailed information about them to the error log. To view recent deadlock events, you can run:

```
sudo tail -n 50 /var/log/mysql/error.log
```

This log output includes information on the transactions involved, the resources they were waiting on, and the SQL statements that were executing at the time of the deadlock. By analyzing these logs, we can determine the root cause of the conflict and identify problematic queries or patterns.

Another useful command is:

```
SHOW ENGINE INNODB STATUS\G
```

This command provides a snapshot of the current InnoDB engine status, including deadlock information. Within the output, you can locate the "LATEST DETECTED DEADLOCK" section, which outlines the transactions involved, the locks held, and the queries that triggered the deadlock. This detailed breakdown allows you to pinpoint which parts of our application need attention.

Resolving Deadlocks

Analyze Deadlock Report

When a deadlock occurs, we start by carefully analyzing the deadlock report from the error log or InnoDB status output. Here, you start looking for:

- The SQL statements involved.
- The specific rows or tables that were locked.
- The order in which locks were acquired.
- The resources each transaction was waiting for.

Once you understand this info, you can spot patterns, like transactions that acquire locks in different orders.

Modify Application Logic

Often, deadlocks can be mitigated by altering the sequence in which transactions access resources. For instance, if you notice that two transactions consistently lock tables in different orders, you can modify our application code to ensure that all transactions acquire locks in the same predefined order.

Let us consider the following example:

- Before Modification, the Transaction A as below:

```
START TRANSACTION;
UPDATE orders SET total_amount = total_amount + 10 WHERE
order_id = 101;
UPDATE inventory SET stock = stock - 1 WHERE product_id = 205;
COMMIT;
```

- And, the Transaction B as below:

```
START TRANSACTION;
UPDATE inventory SET stock = stock - 1 WHERE product_id = 205;
UPDATE orders SET total_amount = total_amount + 10 WHERE
order_id = 101;
COMMIT;
```

After Modification, we enforce a consistent order across transactions. Both Transaction A and Transaction B update the **orders** table first, then the **inventory** table:

```
START TRANSACTION;
UPDATE orders SET total_amount = total_amount + 10 WHERE
order_id = 101;
```

```
UPDATE inventory SET stock = stock - 1 WHERE product_id = 205;
COMMIT;
```

Use Locking Hints and Lower Isolation Levels

In some cases, we can provide explicit locking hints to control the behavior of transactions. For example, using the **FOR UPDATE** clause in a SELECT statement ensures that the rows returned are locked for subsequent updates:

```
START TRANSACTION;
SELECT * FROM orders WHERE order_id = 101 FOR UPDATE;
-- perform the update
COMMIT;
```

Additionally, lowering the transaction isolation level (e.g., from REPEATABLE READ to READ COMMITTED) can reduce the scope and duration of locks, thereby decreasing the chance of deadlocks. However, this must be balanced with the need for data consistency.

Implement Retry Logic

Despite best efforts, deadlocks can still occur. A common practice is to implement retry logic in our application code. When a deadlock is detected, the application can catch the error, wait for a short random interval, and then retry the transaction. Given below is an example in pseudo-code:

```
def execute_transaction(transaction_sql):
    for attempt in range(max_retries):
        try:
            # Begin transaction
            execute_sql("START TRANSACTION;")
            # Execute transaction SQL statements
            execute_sql(transaction_sql)
            # Commit transaction
            execute_sql("COMMIT;")
            return "Transaction successful"
        except DeadlockError:
```

```
            # Rollback in case of deadlock
            execute_sql("ROLLBACK;")
            sleep(random.uniform(0.5, 2.0))
    raise Exception("Transaction failed after retries")
```

This helps make sure that any temporary hiccups don't mess up the big picture and that transactions get done after a quick wait.

These steps helped us deal with the problems that came up when things didn't work right. We figured out how to spot these problems by keeping an eye on error logs and InnoDB status reports. We also came up with some practical solutions, like changing the order of transactions, using locking hints, and setting up retry logic. All of these helped us keep our data consistent and make sure everything was running smoothly in our GitforGits application.

Summary

Together, our GitforGits application helped us get better at SQL by letting us try out advanced analytical techniques and strong transaction control. We began by executing Common Table Expressions (CTEs), including both recursive CTEs and correlated subqueries to break down complex queries into simpler parts and handle hierarchical data with ease. Next, we added window functions like ROW_NUMBER, RANK, LAG, and LEAD to our analytical toolbox.

Continuing our chapter, we carefully managed transactions and learned how to use the START TRANSACTION, COMMIT, and ROLLBACK commands correctly. We added savepoints so that partial rollbacks could be done. We tried out different levels of isolation to find the best balance between concurrency and data integrity. We also changed session and global settings to avoid conflicts during high-volume operations. When transaction conflicts and deadlocks occurred, we analyzed error logs and used InnoDB status reports to identify problematic queries. Then, to effectively resolve these conflicts, we changed our transaction sequences, used locking hints, and added retry logic.

Our comprehensive approach to advanced SQL and transaction control enabled us to handle complex operations confidently for scaling our GitforGits application and supporting future business growth.

Chapter 10: Troubleshoot and Improve Continuously

Overview

This chapter will teach you how to fix problems in our MySQL environment and keep making it better. This will help our GitforGits application stay strong and work well. We will begin by diagnosing slow queries using tools like MySQL Workbench and the EXPLAIN command to pinpoint performance bottlenecks that impact query execution. We will be able to make changes that speed up data retrieval and lower latency if you understand these metrics.

The next step is to deal with replication problems. Here, you will learn how to find and fix problems in how data is synced between nodes. This includes looking at error logs and using SHOW SLAVE STATUS to find configuration errors or network problems, and then using specific commands to get data flowing normally again. We will also learn how to fix storage problems by finding fragmentation, inefficient data types, and settings that aren't set up right. We will improve table structures, rebuild indexes, and fine-tune configuration parameters through hands-on exercises to make sure that our database works well.

Finally, you will tackle configuration challenges, learning how to review and update MySQL settings to prevent performance issues. We will have a complete set of tools by the end of this chapter that you can use to find, fix, and avoid a wide range of problems. This will help make sure that our MySQL environment can consistently and reliably meet the changing needs of our application.

Diagnose Slow Queries

Slow Query on Order History

Imagine that during peak hours, our order history report—designed to retrieve all orders for a given customer—is running much slower than expected. A typical query might look like this:

```
SELECT o.order_id, o.order_date, o.total_amount, c.name
FROM orders o
JOIN customers c ON o.customer_id = c.customer_id
WHERE c.customer_id = 101
ORDER BY o.order_date DESC;
```

We open MySQL Workbench and run the above query. The "Query Analyzer" feature immediately flags this query as slow. The "Top Queries" report indicates that this query has a high average execution time during peak periods.

We click the "Explain" button to generate an execution plan. The plan reveals that the query is performing a full table scan on the **orders** table because the **customer_id** column is not indexed optimally. We also notice that the join between **orders** and **customers** is not as efficient as it could be, resulting in unnecessary row scanning.

So here, based on these insights, we add a composite index on the **orders** table to cover both **customer_id** and **order_date**:

```
ALTER TABLE orders ADD INDEX idx_customer_order (customer_id, order_date);
```

After applying the index, we run the query again. The EXPLAIN output now shows that the index is used effectively, and our execution time drops significantly.

Inefficient Aggregation Query

Another common scenario in our project is an aggregation query used for generating sales summaries. Suppose we have a query to calculate the total sales per day for the last month:

```
SELECT order_date, SUM(total_amount) AS daily_sales

FROM orders

WHERE order_date BETWEEN '2024-03-01' AND '2024-03-31'

GROUP BY order_date;
```

In the Performance Reports section of MySQL Workbench, we've noticed that this query takes longer on days with higher sales volumes. We think that as the number of orders goes up, the query becomes more demanding. When we run EXPLAIN on this query, we see that a temporary table is being created for the grouping operation, and a file sort is used to order the results. This suggests that the query isn't using indexes well for aggregation.

We also observe that the **order_date** column, although filtered in the WHERE clause, is not part of a covering index that includes **total_amount**. As a result, MySQL is forced to scan many rows and then perform aggregation, leading to increased disk I/O. So here, we modify the schema to create an index that covers both columns:

```
ALTER TABLE orders ADD INDEX idx_date_amount (order_date, total_amount);
```

After adding this index, we run the aggregation query again. The execution plan now shows that MySQL can use the index for both filtering and grouping, which drastically reduces the need for temporary tables and file sorts. Our benchmarks confirm that the query execution time has improved noticeably. This scenario demonstrates the importance of understanding data distribution and creating composite indexes to optimize aggregation queries.

Deadlock and Query Conflict Issues

Sometimes, slow queries are symptomatic of underlying transaction conflicts, such as deadlocks, which cause queries to hang or time out. Consider a scenario where multiple concurrent transactions attempt to update inventory records simultaneously.

During peak transaction periods, our monitoring tools and MySQL Workbench's error log display deadlock warnings. Running **SHOW ENGINE INNODB STATUS\G** reveals detailed deadlock information, including which queries were involved and the order of locked resources. We identify that two transactions are updating the **inventory** table in different orders. For example, one transaction updates the **orders** table first, then **inventory**, while another does the reverse. This discrepancy leads to cyclic dependencies and deadlocks.

To resolve this, we standardize the order in which tables are accessed in our transactions. We modify our application logic so that every transaction first updates the **orders** table, followed by the **inventory** table:

```
START TRANSACTION;

UPDATE orders SET total_amount = total_amount + 10 WHERE
order_id = 101;

UPDATE inventory SET stock = stock - 1 WHERE product_id = 205;

COMMIT;
```

Additionally, we implement retry logic to automatically handle any deadlocks that still occur. This real-life example shows that diagnosing slow queries often involves addressing concurrency issues, which can be resolved by ensuring consistent transaction ordering and incorporating retry mechanisms.

Analyzing Multi-Join Queries

In complex reports, we might join multiple large tables, which can result in slow queries if not optimized. Consider a query that joins **orders**, **order_items**, and **products** to generate a detailed sales report:

```
SELECT o.order_id, o.order_date, p.product_name, oi.quantity,
oi.price

FROM orders o

JOIN order_items oi ON o.order_id = oi.order_id

JOIN products p ON oi.product_id = p.product_id

WHERE o.order_date >= '2024-01-01';
```

We observe that this query consumes high CPU and memory resources during execution. The Performance Reports in MySQL Workbench indicate significant disk I/O, suggesting that the join operations are not optimized. Running EXPLAIN shows that some joins are not using indexes effectively, leading to full table scans on large tables. For instance, the join between **order_items** and **products** might be lacking a proper index on the **product_id** column.

Here, we address this by creating appropriate indexes on the join columns:

```
ALTER TABLE order_items ADD INDEX idx_order_id (order_id);
ALTER TABLE products ADD INDEX idx_product_id (product_id);
```

After adding these indexes, we re-run the query and review the EXPLAIN plan. The plan now indicates that indexes are used for all join operations, and resource usage is significantly reduced. This scenario emphasizes that slow multi-join queries can often be resolved by ensuring that all relevant columns are indexed properly, thereby reducing unnecessary table scans and lowering system load.

Resolve Replication Challenges

Common Replication Issues

Before diving into troubleshooting, we review some common replication challenges:

- Misconfigured server IDs, incorrect replication settings, or outdated connection parameters can prevent replication from initializing.
- Unstable network connections may cause replication channels to drop, leading to lag or complete replication stoppage.
- In multi master or multi-source replication, conflicting transactions might cause errors that disrupt the data flow.
- Corruption in binary logs or relay logs can lead to replication failures.
- Incorrect privileges for replication users can block slave nodes from connecting to the master.

These above issues help us quickly narrow down potential causes when replication errors occur.

Identifying Replication Errors

Checking Error Logs

The first step in troubleshooting replication is to examine the MySQL error log. On our Ubuntu server, we run:

```
sudo tail -n 50 /var/log/mysql/error.log
```

This command shows recent error messages, including any replication-related errors. Look for keywords such as "replication," "deadlock," or "failed to connect" to identify issues.

Using SHOW SLAVE STATUS

On slave nodes, we run:

```
SHOW SLAVE STATUS\G
```

This command provides detailed information about the replication process. Key fields to monitor include:

- **Slave_IO_Running:** Indicates if the slave is successfully reading from the master.
- **Slave_SQL_Running:** Shows if the slave is executing the replicated statements.
- **Last_Error:** Contains the most recent error message, which is invaluable for diagnosis.
- **Seconds_Behind_Master:** Displays replication lag; a high number might indicate network or performance issues.

These details help us pinpoint whether the issue lies in the I/O thread, the SQL thread, or the network connection between master and slave.

Troubleshooting Techniques

Resolve Configuration Mismatches

If the error logs or SHOW SLAVE STATUS indicate configuration issues—such as mismatched server IDs or incorrect GTID settings—we review the MySQL configuration files on both master and slave nodes. Ensure that:

- Each node has a unique **`server_id`**.
- GTID mode is enabled and consistent across all nodes.
- Replication settings like **`log_bin`**, **`binlog_format`**, and **`enforce_gtid_consistency`** are properly set.

After making adjustments, restart the MySQL service:

```
sudo systemctl restart mysql
```

Then, re-run SHOW SLAVE STATUS to verify that configuration errors are resolved.

Address Network and Connection Issues

If replication errors are caused by network interruptions, we check connectivity between nodes using ping or telnet commands:

```
ping master_node_ip
telnet master_node_ip 3306
```

These tests help confirm that the network is stable and that MySQL is accessible on the correct port. We also review firewall settings and ensure that required ports for replication (e.g., 3306, 33061 for Group Replication) are open.

Repairing Log File Corruption

Occasionally, replication stops due to corruption in binary logs or relay logs. In such cases, we can reset the slave's relay log by running:

```
STOP SLAVE;
RESET SLAVE ALL;
START SLAVE;
```

This command clears the existing relay logs and forces the slave to re-establish replication from the master's current position. Always back up logs before resetting them, so that you can refer back if needed.

Handling Data Conflicts

In multi master or multi-source replication, conflicting transactions may occur. If a conflict is detected, the error message typically specifies which transaction failed. We then need to:

- Identify the conflicting transactions by examining the binary logs on the master using **`mysqlbinlog`**.
- Resolve conflicts by manually updating the data or adjusting application logic to prevent similar conflicts in the future.
- In some cases, a partial or full rollback on the slave might be necessary to re-align the data with the master.

Once conflicts are resolved, restart replication and monitor the status.

Implementing Automated Recovery Mechanisms

To minimize downtime, we implement automated recovery mechanisms. For example, adding retry logic to the replication process in our application can help handle temporary network glitches. Additionally, configuring MySQL InnoDB Cluster with MySQL Router offers automated failover, reducing the manual intervention required during replication disruptions.

Sample Program: Resolving a Replication Error

Consider a scenario where the slave's SHOW SLAVE STATUS output indicates that the I/O thread is not running due to a connection timeout:

```
Slave_IO_Running: No

Last_Error: error connecting to master 'repl@master_node:3306'
- retry-time: 60  Socket error: Connection timed out
```

We first verify network connectivity from the slave to the master using:

```
ping master_node_ip

telnet master_node_ip 3306
```

If these commands fail, we look into network issues, such as firewall misconfigurations or network outages.

If connectivity appears fine, we examine the replication configuration on the slave. We run:

```
SHOW VARIABLES LIKE 'master_host';
```

to ensure the master's IP is correct. If it is outdated or incorrect, we update the slave's configuration using CHANGE MASTER TO:

```
CHANGE MASTER TO MASTER_HOST='correct_master_ip',
MASTER_USER='repl', MASTER_PASSWORD='StrongReplicatePass!',
MASTER_AUTO_POSITION=1;
```

After updating the configuration, we run:

```
STOP SLAVE;

START SLAVE;
```

Then, we check the status again with SHOW SLAVE STATUS to confirm that the I/O thread is now running.

When we had problems, we'd figure out what was going on by checking error logs, making sure the network was working, fixing log corruption, and dealing with data conflicts. We learned how to fix replication errors quickly. We also set up automated recovery mechanisms and kept an eye on things to make sure our system had a steady flow of data, even when there were some interruptions.

Address Storage Anomalies

Storage Anomalies Overview

There are a few things that can cause problems with storage, like issues with the database files, tables, and indexes. Here are some of the most common issues:

- Over time, frequent data modifications can fragment tables and indexes, causing slower disk reads and inefficient space usage.
- Using data types that consume more storage than necessary can lead to bloated tables and increased memory overhead.
- Improper configuration of parameters like **innodb_file_per_table** or buffer sizes can lead to suboptimal disk I/O performance.
- Residual files from deleted or altered tables might occupy valuable disk space and hinder performance.

These anomalies are the first step toward resolving them to have our database remain responsive and maintain data integrity.

Detecting Storage Anomalies

Monitoring Table and Index Fragmentation

We begin by checking table status using MySQL's INFORMATION_SCHEMA to gauge fragmentation. For example, we execute:

```
SELECT table_name, data_length, index_length, data_free
FROM information_schema.tables
WHERE table_schema = 'bookdepot';
```

The **data_free** column indicates unused space within tables, which can signal fragmentation. High values may prompt further assessment.

Reviewing Log Files and System Metrics

We monitor system logs for error messages related to disk I/O or file system issues. Using:

```
sudo tail -n 50 /var/log/mysql/error.log
```

we look for warnings that might indicate underlying storage problems. Additionally, we use tools like **iostat** and **vmstat** to monitor disk performance at the operating system level, ensuring that hardware issues are not contributing to storage anomalies.

Correcting Storage Anomalies

Rebuilding Fragmented Tables and Indexes

To reduce fragmentation, we use the **OPTIMIZE TABLE** command. For example, if the **orders** table shows significant free space, we execute:

```
OPTIMIZE TABLE orders;
```

This command rebuilds the table and indexes, reclaiming unused space and improving I/O efficiency. We perform similar operations on other tables identified with high fragmentation.

Adjusting Data Types for Efficiency

Inefficient data types can bloat table sizes. We audit our schema and adjust columns where necessary. For instance, if a **TEXT** field only ever stores short strings, we modify it to a **VARCHAR** with an appropriate length:

```
ALTER TABLE products MODIFY COLUMN description VARCHAR(255);
```

This change not only reduces storage requirements but also improves index performance by reducing overhead.

Enabling innodb_file_per_table

Using the **innodb_file_per_table** setting can improve storage management by storing each InnoDB table in its own file. We check our MySQL configuration file and ensure that this setting is enabled:

```
[mysqld]
innodb_file_per_table = 1
```

After updating, we restart MySQL:

```
sudo systemctl restart mysql
```

This setup simplifies maintenance tasks, as individual tables can be optimized or backed up without affecting the entire database.

Archiving Old Data

To manage growing data volumes, we implement archiving strategies for data that is infrequently accessed. For instance, we can partition the **orders** table by year and then archive older partitions.

```
ALTER TABLE orders DROP PARTITION p2020;
```

The archiving helps to keep the primary database lean and ensures that queries remain fast.

Beyond these such database-level adjustments, we ensure that our underlying hardware and file system are optimized. Placing the MySQL data directory on SSDs and configuring RAID (e.g., RAID 10) improves disk performance and reliability.

We also collaborate with system administrators to tune the operating system's I/O scheduler for optimal performance, for instance:

```
echo deadline | sudo tee /sys/block/sda/queue/scheduler
```

This command sets the I/O scheduler to "deadline," which is often recommended for SSDs handling heavy database workloads.

Integrating Corrections into Application

Testing Impact of Corrections

After applying the above corrections, we re-run our initial diagnostic queries to compare storage metrics. We use:

```
SELECT table_name, data_length, index_length, data_free
FROM information_schema.tables
WHERE table_schema = 'bookdepot';
```

This lets us verify that the **data_free** space has decreased, indicating successful defragmentation. We also re-check performance reports in MySQL Workbench to ensure that disk I/O metrics have improved.

Continuous Monitoring and Maintenance

To sustain optimal storage performance, we establish a routine for ongoing monitoring. We set up scheduled jobs to run **OPTIMIZE TABLE** during off-peak hours, and we configure alerts using monitoring tools like Prometheus to notify us of any sudden increases in **data_free** or abnormal disk I/O patterns. This proactive maintenance ensures that storage anomalies are addressed promptly before they impact system performance.

Fix Configuration Challenges

Now let's talk about some of the common configuration problems that can mess with the performance of our MySQL 9 setup for GitforGits. These problems can happen because of incorrect settings in the configuration file, outdated parameters, or human error when tuning. If we can find these misconfigurations and use the right commands, we can get the MySQL settings back on track and make sure our database is running smoothly.

Identifying Configuration Issues

Before making changes, we first need to identify potential misconfigurations. These issues may manifest as slow query performance, high resource consumption, or even instability in the database. To diagnose problems, we review key MySQL settings in the configuration file and compare them against best practices and our current workload requirements.

We begin by checking vital parameters such as:

- Is innodb_buffer_pool_size sized appropriately for our available RAM and workload?
- Are we allowing too many or too few connections?
- Is **log_bin and binlog_format** settings correctly enabled for replication and recovery?
- Are **`gtid_mode`** and **`enforce_gtid_consistency`** correctly configured to support our replication strategies?

We also review system logs and error messages using:

```
sudo tail -n 50 /var/log/mysql/error.log
```

If we do all this, it gives us clues about misconfigurations, such as warnings about insufficient buffer sizes or deprecated options.

Misconfigurations Impact?

Insufficient Memory Allocation

One frequent issue is an undersized InnoDB buffer pool. If the buffer pool is too small, the system will rely heavily on disk I/O, causing slow query responses and increased latency. For example, setting **`innodb_buffer_pool_size`** too low for a dedicated database server can lead to excessive swapping and degraded performance.

Incorrect Connection Settings

Another common misconfiguration is setting an inappropriate number for **`max_connections`**. If set too high, the server might allocate excessive resources for idle connections, reducing available memory for active queries. Conversely, setting it too low may prevent legitimate connections during peak usage.

Misconfigured Binary Logging

Improper binary logging settings can disrupt replication and recovery. For instance, an incorrect **binlog_format** or failure to enable **gtid_mode** might cause replication errors or make it difficult to recover from a crash.

Outdated or Deprecated Parameters

Over time, certain configuration options become deprecated. Using outdated parameters may not only generate warnings but can also lead to unexpected behavior. Regularly updating our configuration file to align with MySQL 9 best practices is crucial.

Fixing Configuration Issues

Review and Update Configuration File

We start by opening the MySQL configuration file and then systematically review key settings. First, we assess the current value of **innodb_buffer_pool_size** and adjust it based on available system RAM. For a dedicated MySQL server with 16GB of RAM, we might set:

```
innodb_buffer_pool_size = 10G
```

- Connection Settings:

Next, we evaluate **max_connections** and other related settings. If our workload demands it, we can set:

```
max_connections = 300
thread_cache_size = 50
```

- Binary Logging and GTID Configuration:

We ensure that replication settings are correctly enabled:

```
log_bin = mysql-bin
binlog_format = ROW
gtid_mode = ON
enforce_gtid_consistency = ON
```

- Other Settings:

We check additional parameters such as query cache settings (if applicable) and adjust file-per-table settings:

```
innodb_file_per_table = 1
```

After making the necessary updates, we save the file and exit the editor.

Restart MySQL to Apply Changes

To ensure that our changes take effect, we restart the MySQL service:

```
sudo systemctl restart mysql
```

After the restart, we verify that the service is running without errors:

```
sudo systemctl status mysql
```

Validate Changes with SHOW VARIABLES

We log into the MySQL shell to confirm that the configuration parameters are set as intended:

```
mysql -u root -p
SHOW VARIABLES LIKE 'innodb_buffer_pool_size';
SHOW VARIABLES LIKE 'max_connections';
SHOW VARIABLES LIKE 'gtid_mode';
```

This step confirms that our updates are correctly applied and gives us a clear picture of the current configuration.

Monitor System Performance

Using MySQL Workbench, we review performance reports and dashboards to check the impact of our configuration changes. For example, we monitor the InnoDB buffer pool hit ratio:

```
SHOW GLOBAL STATUS LIKE 'Innodb_buffer_pool_read_hits';
```

A high hit ratio indicates that most read operations are served from memory, confirming the effectiveness of our memory allocation. We also observe metrics like CPU and disk I/O usage, ensuring that our system operates within optimal parameters.

Address Specific Configuration Errors

Suppose our error log revealed issues with binary logging. For example, if we saw an error like "GTID consistency check failed," we would double-check the relevant settings. In such cases, targeted commands can resolve these issues. For example, if the **gtid_mode** wasn't properly enabled, we might execute:

```
SET GLOBAL gtid_mode = ON;
SET GLOBAL enforce_gtid_consistency = ON;
```

After running these commands, we recheck with SHOW VARIABLES to ensure the settings are applied.

Apply Automated Configuration Checks

To prevent future misconfigurations, we can create automated scripts that periodically check critical MySQL settings. A simple bash script might connect to MySQL and compare current variable values against our expected benchmarks:

```
#!/bin/bash
mysql -u root -pYourPassword -e "SHOW VARIABLES LIKE
'innodb_buffer_pool_size';" > /path/to/check.log
```

We schedule this script via cron to run daily, alerting us if any value deviates from our optimal configuration. This proactive monitoring helps us maintain a consistent and efficient environment.

Preventive Measures and Best Practices

Regular Reviews and Updates

We established that database workloads evolve over time. Regularly reviewing and updating our MySQL configuration is essential. We schedule periodic audits of our configuration file and cross-check with the latest MySQL 9 documentation to ensure we are not using deprecated parameters.

Documentation of Configuration Changes

Maintaining clear documentation of all configuration changes, including the rationale behind each setting, is crucial. This documentation serves as a reference for troubleshooting and future optimizations, ensuring that team members are aligned on best practices.

Collaboration with System Administrators

In many cases, misconfigurations may arise from hardware or network settings rather than MySQL itself. We work closely with system administrators to ensure that the underlying operating system and storage configurations (such as I/O scheduler settings or RAID configurations) are optimized to complement our MySQL settings.

The above optimized settings led to improved system performance, reduced resource contention, and enhanced stability. This whole strategy improves our current setup and builds skills and processes needed to maintain a high-performing, scalable MySQL environment over the long term.

Summary

In short, we went over many different aspects of fixing problems and making our MySQL environment better all the time for the GitforGits application. First, we used MySQL Workbench and the EXPLAIN command to figure out why queries were running slowly. Then, we targeted optimizations like re-indexing and query rewrites were put in place. We looked into replication errors by keeping an eye on error logs and using SHOW SLAVE STATUS. Because of this, we made changes to our replication settings and automated recovery systems to make sure that data kept moving between nodes.

To fix storage problems, we found fragmentation and inefficient data types and fixed them by using OPTIMIZE TABLE commands and changing the definitions of the tables to free up disk space and speed up I/O. Also, we looked over our MySQL configuration and found parameters that were set incorrectly. We then used specific commands to update settings like innodb_buffer_pool_size and max_connections, which restored optimal performance. This extensive hands-on experience made it easier for us to keep up a strong, high-performing database environment that could adapt to changing operational needs.

CHAPTER 11: AUTOMATE DATABASE WORKFLOWS

Overview

In order to decrease manual intervention and increase operational efficiency for the GitforGits application, you will discover in this chapter how to automate our database workflows. We will learn a variety of ways to automate tasks, starting with writing shell scripts that run important MySQL commands for maintenance, backups, and data cleanup. We will then configure scheduled events within MySQL to run these tasks automatically at predefined intervals.

Additionally, you will connect MySQL to outside programs like Google Spreadsheets, Google Docs, and AWS S3. This will let you export data for group reporting and store backups safely for disaster recovery. We will learn how to make a strong, automated framework that makes day-to-day database management easier by working with real-world examples.

Upon completion of this chapter, you will have created a thorough automation plan that not only maintains high performance and reliability but also frees up valuable time for more important, strategic tasks. This will ensure that our MySQL environment can easily adapt to the changing needs of our application.

Explore Database Automation

We also need to think around automating the repetitive operations such as backups, maintenance tasks, data cleanup, and performance monitoring so that our team can focus on higher-level tasks. So, we will look after some of the practical techniques for setting up automated workflows and introduce supplementary tools that enhance our automation capabilities.

Streamlining Routine Maintenance Tasks

As our database grows, routine maintenance tasks become increasingly time-consuming if performed manually. We plan to automate several key activities to ensure our environment remains optimized. Simply, we can automate backup operations using command-line tools in combination with scheduled cron jobs.

For example, we can write a shell script to dump the database and then schedule it to run nightly:

```
#!/bin/bash
DATE=$(date +%F)
mysqldump -u root -p'YourPassword' bookdepot >
/backup/bookdepot_backup_$DATE.sql
```

Another thing is that over time, tables and indexes may become fragmented, leading to degraded performance. We can automate the execution of commands like **OPTIMIZE TABLE** and periodic index rebuilding via scheduled events or cron jobs, ensuring that our data remains well-organized and responsive.

Also, to manage disk space and maintain optimal performance, we will set up automated routines to clean up outdated logs and archive historical data. For example, an event can be created to purge log entries older than 30 days.

Now so far, you have already upskilled in using MySQL Workbench for performance monitoring, but now we can also try to leverage its advanced scheduling and scripting capabilities to automate repetitive tasks. We can learn how to configure scheduled SQL scripts within the Workbench environment to trigger routine operations. These tasks may include, creating scheduled reports that extract key performance metrics and deliver them via email or dashboard updates, and automating scripts that perform routine maintenance tasks such as re-indexing, statistics updates, and partition management.

Supplementary Tools for Enhanced Automation

Beyond the capabilities within MySQL Workbench, we will explore additional tools to further streamline our database workflows:

Cron Jobs and Shell Scripting

Cron jobs provide a reliable way to schedule scripts on a Linux system. We will write shell scripts to automate various tasks:

- As demonstrated earlier, a shell script can run **`mysqldump`** at scheduled intervals.
- Scripts can be created to archive old logs and remove unnecessary files, ensuring that disk space is managed effectively.
- Automated routines can remove obsolete or redundant data from specific tables based on defined criteria.

Configuration Management and Orchestration Tools

In larger, more complex environments, tools like Ansible, Chef, or Puppet can be used to automate the deployment and configuration of MySQL instances. We will explore how to write configuration playbooks that ensure consistency across multiple servers. For example, an Ansible playbook might handle:

- Automating the installation of MySQL, setting parameters like **`innodb_buffer_pool_size`**, and configuring replication.
- Scheduling tasks like backups and index optimizations across the entire cluster.
- Running regular audits of configuration settings and applying corrective measures when deviations are detected.

Integrating with Monitoring and Alerting Systems

We can do the integration of monitoring and alerting systems to keep track of scheduled tasks and overall system health. Tools such as Prometheus and Grafana can be set up to monitor key performance metrics and trigger alerts when thresholds are exceeded.

For instance:

- Automated alerts can notify the team if a scheduled backup fails.
- Monitoring dashboards can provide real-time insights into disk I/O, query performance, and resource utilization, prompting timely interventions if any anomaly is detected.

These monitoring systems with our automated workflows having successfully integrated may help to identify the issues and get them addressed before they escalate.

Designing Comprehensive Automation Workflow

Map Out Routine Tasks

We begin by documenting all the routine tasks that currently require manual intervention. This includes tasks like:

- Database backups
- Index optimization
- Log rotation and cleanup
- Data archiving
- Performance reporting

This mapping provides clarity on which tasks should be automated and sets the foundation for our automation strategy.

Develop and Test Automation Scripts

Next, we develop automation scripts for each task. Each script is rigorously tested in a development or staging environment to ensure it executes correctly and doesn't interfere with other operations. We refine the scripts based on test results, ensuring they handle error conditions gracefully and provide meaningful log output.

Schedule and Deploy

Once validated, we deploy these scripts in our production environment using cron jobs or event schedulers. We set up the scheduling to minimize impact on peak usage times. For example, backups and index optimizations might run during late-night hours when the load is low.

Monitor and Iterate

Finally, we establish a continuous monitoring routine to track the performance and success of our automated tasks. We integrate logging and alerting to notify us if any scheduled task fails or if performance metrics deviate from expected norms. This iterative process allows us to refine our automation workflows over time, ensuring they adapt to changes in data volume and system load.

Develop Shell Scripts

Shell scripts are an effective way to automate repetitive tasks in a Linux environment. They allow us to bundle multiple commands into a single executable file, which can be scheduled via cron or executed manually when needed. In our context or for our application, shell scripts will help us:

- Perform regular backups without manual initiation.
- Execute maintenance commands such as index rebuilding or table optimization.
- Run custom MySQL queries and export reports.
- Log operations and errors for further analysis.

With shell scripts, we make sure that our database operations are done the same way every time. This helps reduce the risk of human error and makes the system more reliable.

Automating MySQL Backups

One of the most critical tasks is ensuring that our data is backed up regularly. Below is an example shell script that performs a complete backup of our GitforGits Book Depot database using **`mysqldump`**.

Following is the sample backup script:

```
#!/bin/bash

# Script: backup_mysql.sh

# Purpose: Perform a complete backup of the GitforGits Book
Depot database

# Configuration Variables

DB_USER="root"

DB_PASSWORD="YourPassword"  # Consider using a secure method
to store passwords

DB_NAME="bookdepot"

BACKUP_DIR="/backup"

DATE=$(date +%F)

BACKUP_FILE="${BACKUP_DIR}/${DB_NAME}_backup_${DATE}.sql"
```

```
# Create backup directory if it doesn't exist
if [ ! -d "${BACKUP_DIR}" ]; then
    mkdir -p "${BACKUP_DIR}"
fi
# Perform the backup
echo "Starting backup for ${DB_NAME} at ${DATE}..."
mysqldump -u ${DB_USER} -p${DB_PASSWORD} ${DB_NAME} >
${BACKUP_FILE}
# Check if backup was successful
if [ $? -eq 0 ]; then
    echo "Backup successful: ${BACKUP_FILE}"
else
    echo "Backup failed!" >&2
fi
```

In the above script, we define variables for the database user, password, database name, and backup directory. Using variables makes the script easily adaptable. The script checks if the backup directory exists and creates it if necessary.

Also, the **mysqldump** command is executed with the specified parameters, and the output is redirected to a file named with the current date. This helps in organizing backups chronologically. The script checks the exit status of the **mysqldump** command to confirm whether the backup was successful and logs the outcome.

Running Maintenance Tasks

Another essential set of tasks involves routine maintenance such as optimizing tables, rebuilding indexes, and cleaning up outdated logs. The following script automates these tasks for our GitforGits Book Depot database.

Following is the maintenance script”

```
#!/bin/bash
# Script: maintenance_mysql.sh
# Purpose: Run routine maintenance tasks on the GitforGits
Book Depot database
```

```
# Configuration Variables
DB_USER="root"
DB_PASSWORD="YourPassword"
DB_NAME="bookdepot"
LOG_FILE="/var/log/mysql/maintenance.log"
# Function to log messages
log_message() {
    echo "$(date +'%F %T') - $1" >> ${LOG_FILE}
}
# Optimize Tables
optimize_tables() {
    log_message "Starting table optimization..."
    mysql -u ${DB_USER} -p${DB_PASSWORD} -e "USE ${DB_NAME};
SHOW TABLES;" | while read table; do
        # Skip header line
        if [[ "${table}" != "Tables_in_${DB_NAME}" ]]; then
            log_message "Optimizing table: ${table}"
            mysql -u ${DB_USER} -p${DB_PASSWORD} -e "OPTIMIZE
TABLE ${DB_NAME}.${table};" >> ${LOG_FILE} 2>&1
        fi
    done
    log_message "Table optimization completed."
}
# Rebuild Indexes (if necessary)
rebuild_indexes() {
    log_message "Starting index rebuilding..."
    # Example: Rebuild index for a specific table (customize
as needed)
```

```
    mysql -u ${DB_USER} -p${DB_PASSWORD} -e "ALTER TABLE
${DB_NAME}.orders DROP INDEX idx_order_date, ADD INDEX
idx_order_date (order_date);" >> ${LOG_FILE} 2>&1
    log_message "Index rebuilding completed for orders table."
}
# Cleanup Old Logs
cleanup_logs() {
    log_message "Starting log cleanup..."
    # Remove MySQL slow query logs older than 30 days
    find /var/log/mysql/ -type f -name "mysql-slow.log*" -
mtime +30 -exec rm {} \;
    log_message "Log cleanup completed."
}
# Execute Maintenance Tasks
log_message "Maintenance script started."
optimize_tables
rebuild_indexes
cleanup_logs
log_message "Maintenance script completed."
```

Here, a function (**log_message**) is defined to append timestamped messages to a log file. This aids in tracking the execution of maintenance tasks. The **optimize_tables** function retrieves a list of tables from the database and runs the **OPTIMIZE TABLE** command on each. This operation defragments tables and reclaims unused space.

The script includes an example of dropping and recreating an index on the **orders** table. This step can be customized for other tables and indexes as needed. The **cleanup_logs** function uses the **find** command to locate and delete MySQL slow query logs older than 30 days, thereby managing disk space. The script logs the start and end of maintenance, running each function in sequence.

Combining Tasks into a Unified Workflow

To streamline our automation further, we can combine backup and maintenance scripts into a single unified workflow. This approach allows us to perform a full maintenance cycle, including backups, optimizations, and cleanup, in one scheduled job.

Below is a quick unified workflow script:

```
#!/bin/bash
# Script: full_maintenance.sh
# Purpose: Perform full maintenance tasks including backup,
optimization, and cleanup
# Configuration Variables
DB_USER="root"
DB_PASSWORD="YourPassword"
DB_NAME="bookdepot"
BACKUP_DIR="/backup"
LOG_FILE="/var/log/mysql/full_maintenance.log"
DATE=$(date +%F)
BACKUP_FILE="${BACKUP_DIR}/${DB_NAME}_backup_${DATE}.sql"
# Function to log messages
log_message() {
    echo "$(date +'%F %T') - $1" >> ${LOG_FILE}
}
# Create backup directory if it doesn't exist
if [ ! -d "${BACKUP_DIR}" ]; then
    mkdir -p "${BACKUP_DIR}"
fi
log_message "Full maintenance script started."
# Backup Database
log_message "Starting backup for ${DB_NAME}."
mysqldump -u ${DB_USER} -p${DB_PASSWORD} ${DB_NAME} >
${BACKUP_FILE}
if [ $? -eq 0 ]; then
    log_message "Backup successful: ${BACKUP_FILE}"
else
    log_message "Backup failed!" >&2
```

```
fi
# Optimize Tables
log_message "Starting table optimization..."
mysql -u ${DB_USER} -p${DB_PASSWORD} -e "USE ${DB_NAME}; SHOW TABLES;" | while read table; do
    if [[ "${table}" != "Tables_in_${DB_NAME}" ]]; then
        log_message "Optimizing table: ${table}"
        mysql -u ${DB_USER} -p${DB_PASSWORD} -e "OPTIMIZE TABLE ${DB_NAME}.${table};" >> ${LOG_FILE} 2>&1
    fi
done
log_message "Table optimization completed."
# Rebuild Indexes for Orders Table
log_message "Rebuilding index for orders table..."
mysql -u ${DB_USER} -p${DB_PASSWORD} -e "ALTER TABLE ${DB_NAME}.orders DROP INDEX idx_order_date, ADD INDEX idx_order_date (order_date);" >> ${LOG_FILE} 2>&1
log_message "Index rebuilding completed for orders table."
# Cleanup Old Logs
log_message "Starting log cleanup..."
find /var/log/mysql/ -type f -name "mysql-slow.log*" -mtime +30 -exec rm {} \;
log_message "Log cleanup completed."
log_message "Full maintenance script completed."
```

Here, this script consolidates backup, table optimization, index rebuilding, and log cleanup into one workflow, ensuring that all essential maintenance tasks are executed in sequence. The script uses a consistent logging approach to record the start and end of each task. This detailed log file is invaluable for troubleshooting and verifying that each step completes successfully. The backup section includes error checking to ensure that any failure is logged. Additional error handling can be added to other sections as needed. Once tested and refined, this unified script can be scheduled via cron to run during off-peak hours, ensuring that our database remains optimized without manual intervention.

Schedule Events

The scheduled events let us run SQL statements or batches of statements at set times right in the MySQL server. This built-in feature is a lifesaver for things like data cleanup, regular reporting, maintenance, and even kicking off backup procedures. With MySQL's Event Scheduler, we can cut down on manual intervention and make sure critical tasks run smoothly, even during off-peak hours.

Enabling Event Scheduler

Before we can create scheduled events, we need to ensure that the MySQL Event Scheduler is enabled. By default, it might be disabled, so we check its status by executing:

```
SHOW VARIABLES LIKE 'event_scheduler';
```

If the result shows 'OFF', we can enable it temporarily for the current session:

```
SET GLOBAL event_scheduler = ON;
```

For a permanent solution, we add the following line to our MySQL configuration file:

```
event_scheduler = ON
```

After updating the configuration file, a MySQL restart is required:

```
sudo systemctl restart mysql
```

Creating Scheduled Events

Automating Log Cleanup

One common task is cleaning up outdated logs to conserve disk space and maintain optimal performance. For instance, suppose we want to remove entries from the **logs** table that are older than 30 days.

Here, we can create a scheduled event that runs daily to perform this cleanup:

```
CREATE EVENT IF NOT EXISTS cleanup_old_logs
ON SCHEDULE EVERY 1 DAY
STARTS '2024-05-01 02:00:00'
DO
```

```
  DELETE FROM logs WHERE log_date < NOW() - INTERVAL 30 DAY;
```

This event is configured to start at 2 AM on May 1, 2024, and execute every day. The use of **IF NOT EXISTS** ensures that we don't inadvertently create duplicate events.

Periodic Index Rebuilding

Another important maintenance task is rebuilding indexes to reduce fragmentation and improve query performance. Consider a scenario where the **orders** table experiences high update activity, leading to fragmented indexes.

Here, we can schedule an event to optimize the table on a weekly basis:

```
CREATE EVENT IF NOT EXISTS optimize_orders
ON SCHEDULE EVERY 1 WEEK
STARTS '2024-05-01 03:00:00'
DO
  OPTIMIZE TABLE orders;
```

This event runs once a week at 3 AM, ensuring that the table remains defragmented without manual intervention.

Generating Daily Reports

Scheduled events can also be used to generate automated reports. For example, if we need a daily summary of order statistics, we can create an event that inserts the aggregated data into a reporting table:

```
CREATE EVENT IF NOT EXISTS daily_order_summary
ON SCHEDULE EVERY 1 DAY
STARTS '2024-05-01 04:00:00'
DO
  INSERT INTO order_summary (summary_date, total_orders,
total_sales)
  SELECT CURDATE(), COUNT(*), SUM(total_amount)
  FROM orders
  WHERE order_date = CURDATE();
```

This event captures daily order statistics and stores them in the **order_summary** table, allowing for easy historical analysis.

Managing and Monitoring Scheduled Events

Viewing Existing Events

To view all scheduled events in our database, we can run the following query:

```
SHOW EVENTS FROM bookdepot;
```

This command lists details about each event, including their schedule, status, and the last executed time. Monitoring this output helps us verify that our events are running as planned.

Modifying and Dropping Events

If we need to update an event—say, changing the frequency or start time—we use the ALTER EVENT command. For example, to change the daily cleanup event to run at 1 AM instead of 2 AM, we execute:

```
ALTER EVENT cleanup_old_logs
ON SCHEDULE EVERY 1 DAY
STARTS '2024-05-01 01:00:00';
```

To remove an event that is no longer needed, we simply run:

```
DROP EVENT IF EXISTS daily_order_summary;
```

These commands give us control over our automation workflows, ensuring that they can be modified as our requirements evolve.

In the above, the events we create help streamline operations, reduce maintenance overhead, and contribute to a more resilient system. As we integrate these scheduled events into our operational workflow, we continue to monitor their performance and make adjustments as needed.

Integrate External Tools

Integrating MySQL with other tools has some major perks. For starters, you can share and report data in real time, which is crucial for making informed business decisions. For example, you can export data to Google Sheets, allowing non-technical team members to access up-to-date reports without needing direct database access. Additionally, integrating with cloud storage solutions like AWS S3 helps securely archive backups and large datasets, ensuring data durability and easy retrieval. It also makes things easier for team members to work together since they're already used to the platforms and don't have to mess around with the database.

Integration with Google Spreadsheets

Exporting Data from MySQL

One common scenario is the need to export query results from MySQL to a Google Spreadsheet for collaborative reporting. We start by writing a query that extracts the required data. For example, to generate a daily sales report, we might use:

```
SELECT order_date, COUNT(*) AS total_orders, SUM(total_amount)
AS total_sales

FROM orders

WHERE order_date = CURDATE()

GROUP BY order_date;
```

Automating Data Export with a Script

We then create a shell script that runs this query using the **mysql** command-line tool and exports the results into a CSV file:

```
#!/bin/bash

# Script: export_daily_sales.sh

DB_USER="root"

DB_PASSWORD="YourPassword"

DB_NAME="bookdepot"

OUTPUT_FILE="/path/to/daily_sales_$(date +%F).csv"

mysql -u ${DB_USER} -p${DB_PASSWORD} -D ${DB_NAME} -e "SELECT
order_date, COUNT(*) AS total_orders, SUM(total_amount) AS
total_sales FROM orders WHERE order_date = CURDATE() GROUP BY
order_date;" | sed 's/\t/,/g' > ${OUTPUT_FILE}
```

This script extracts the query results, converts tab-separated values to comma-separated values using **sed**, and saves them as a CSV file.

Uploading Data to Google Spreadsheets

Next, we use Google Sheets API to import the CSV file into a spreadsheet. This can be accomplished using Python or other scripting languages.

For example, using Python with the **gspread** and **oauth2client** libraries, we write a script that reads the CSV file and updates a Google Spreadsheet:

```
import csv
import gspread
from oauth2client.service_account import
ServiceAccountCredentials
# Define the scope and authenticate using our credentials JSON
file
scope = ['https://spreadsheets.google.com/feeds',
'https://www.googleapis.com/auth/drive']
creds =
ServiceAccountCredentials.from_json_keyfile_name('path/to/cred
entials.json', scope)
client = gspread.authorize(creds)
# Open the target spreadsheet and select the first worksheet
spreadsheet = client.open("Daily Sales Report")
worksheet = spreadsheet.sheet1
# Read CSV data and update the spreadsheet
with open('/path/to/daily_sales_2024-05-01.csv', 'r') as
csvfile:
    csv_reader = csv.reader(csvfile)
    data = list(csv_reader)
    worksheet.update('A1', data)
```

This script reads the CSV file generated earlier and uploads its contents into a designated Google Spreadsheet, making the data available for collaboration and analysis.

Integration with Google Docs

For teams that prefer narrative reports, we can integrate MySQL with Google Docs to generate automated reports. Using a similar approach as with Google Spreadsheets, we first extract data from MySQL. Then, using the Google Docs API, we generate a document that includes formatted results and insights.

For example, after exporting data, we write a Python script that uses the **google-api-python-client** library to create a new document:

```
from googleapiclient.discovery import build
```

```
from oauth2client.service_account import
ServiceAccountCredentials

# Define scope and authenticate

scope = ['https://www.googleapis.com/auth/documents']

creds =
ServiceAccountCredentials.from_json_keyfile_name('path/to/cred
entials.json', scope)

docs_service = build('docs', 'v1', credentials=creds)

# Create a new document

document = docs_service.documents().create(body={'title':
'Daily Sales Report'}).execute()

document_id = document.get('documentId')

# Insert text content

requests = [
    {
        'insertText': {
            'location': {
                'index': 1,
            },
            'text': 'Daily Sales Report for ' + '2024-05-
01\n\n'
        }
    },
    # Additional requests to insert formatted data can be
added here
]

result =
docs_service.documents().batchUpdate(documentId=document_id,
body={'requests': requests}).execute()
```

This script creates a new Google Doc titled "Daily Sales Report" and inserts initial text. Further requests can be constructed to format and insert detailed data extracted from MySQL.

Integration with AWS Storage

Another important integration is with AWS S3, which can be used for storing automated backups. We already developed shell scripts to create backups; now, we extend them to upload these backups to an S3 bucket.

Configure AWS CLI

First, install and configure the AWS CLI on our server:

```
sudo apt-get install awscli
aws configure
```

Enter our AWS access key, secret key, default region, and output format when prompted.

Modify Backup Script to Upload to S3

We update our backup script to include an S3 upload step:

```
#!/bin/bash
# Script: backup_and_upload.sh
DB_USER="root"
DB_PASSWORD="YourPassword"
DB_NAME="bookdepot"
BACKUP_DIR="/backup"
DATE=$(date +%F)
BACKUP_FILE="${BACKUP_DIR}/${DB_NAME}_backup_${DATE}.sql"
S3_BUCKET="s3://your-s3-bucket/backups/"
# Create backup directory if it doesn't exist
if [ ! -d "${BACKUP_DIR}" ]; then
    mkdir -p "${BACKUP_DIR}"
fi
# Perform the backup
echo "Starting backup for ${DB_NAME} at ${DATE}..."
mysqldump -u ${DB_USER} -p${DB_PASSWORD} ${DB_NAME} >
${BACKUP_FILE}
```

```
# Check if backup was successful
if [ $? -eq 0 ]; then
    echo "Backup successful: ${BACKUP_FILE}"
    # Upload the backup to AWS S3
    aws s3 cp ${BACKUP_FILE} ${S3_BUCKET}
    if [ $? -eq 0 ]; then
        echo "Backup uploaded to S3 successfully."
    else
        echo "Failed to upload backup to S3." >&2
    fi
else
    echo "Backup failed!" >&2
fi
```

This script not only creates a backup of the database but also uploads it to a specified S3 bucket, ensuring that backups are stored off-site for disaster recovery purposes.

All these integrations cut down on manual intervention and make collaboration and data accessibility better. We showed how to automate data export to Google Spreadsheets and Google Docs and how to securely archive backups on AWS S3 using practical examples and detailed steps. Because of this extensive approach to external integration, our team can focus on strategic development. We can be sure that routine tasks are being handled automatically and that our data is both secure and readily available for analysis and recovery.

Summary

Overall, we successfully streamlined our database operations by means of automation of routine workflows. We developed a robust understanding of how to leverage MySQL's built-in scheduling capabilities along with external tools to reduce manual intervention. Our work began with automating essential tasks such as backups, table optimization, and log cleanup through shell scripts. We wrote scripts that executed MySQL commands, performed consistent backups using mysqldump, and optimized tables with the OPTIMIZE TABLE command, ensuring that routine maintenance was handled automatically. We further enhanced our automation strategy by configuring scheduled events within MySQL. These events were designed to trigger specific tasks at predetermined intervals, which not only saved time but also ensured that critical maintenance activities occurred reliably during off-peak hours.

Additionally, we integrated our MySQL environment with external tools such as Google Spreadsheets, Google Docs, and AWS S3. This integration allowed us to automate the export of data for reporting purposes and securely archive backups off-site, thereby enhancing data accessibility and disaster recovery capabilities. Overall, we gained practical skills in scripting, scheduling, and external integration that empowered us to maintain a high-performing, scalable, and resilient MySQL environment.

Index

A

B

C

D

E

F

G

I

L

M

N

O

Epilogue

As I come to the end of this book, I am filled with an overwhelming sense of optimism regarding the practical skills you have acquired to excel in the tasks that you perform on a daily basis as a DBA. MySQL 9 has fundamentally altered the way in which we manage databases, and the strategies that we have discussed will assist you in achieving new levels of productivity in your work operations. As you progressed through this book, you gained the knowledge and skills necessary to install, configure, and optimize MySQL 9. These abilities will provide you with a solid foundation upon which to tackle routine database administration tasks.

I saw for myself how modern techniques like high availability, advanced query optimizations, and replication can make day-to-day tasks more reliable and efficient. Having these skills will allow you to quickly diagnose queries that are running slowly, resolve conflicts that arise from transactions, and keep data integrity intact even when there is a lot of traffic. You will be able to maintain the consistency and accuracy of your data by utilizing the practical methods for managing transactions and balancing isolation levels. This will ensure that essential business operations are carried out without any interruptions. The automation strategies that we looked into are about more than just saving time; they are about constructing a system that functions reliably, day in and day out, without the need for constant intervention from a human being. You are now able to automate backups, maintenance tasks, and even reporting by creating scheduled events and shell scripts within your system. Because of this, you will be able to focus on taking strategic initiatives rather than performing mundane tasks.

In addition, the integration of MySQL with external tools such as cloud storage and collaborative platforms has increased the number of possibilities for data sharing and disaster recovery. You will be able to maintain a database environment that is both secure and high-performing, and that is also capable of adapting to the ever-changing requirements of your business thanks to these integrations. Not only did the implementation of these practices result in an improvement in my day-to-day operations, but it also resulted in a significant reduction in the risk of incidents that were considered to be critical. It is my belief that the knowledge and abilities that you have acquired from reading this book will enable you to construct, maintain, and enhance your MySQL environment with self-assurance and agility.

This book and the learnings you gained are sufficient to ensure that your database continues to be functional, responsive, and prepared for the future.

Thank You

www.ingramcontent.com/pod-product-compliance
Lightning Source LLC
Chambersburg PA
CBHW080213170726
48282CB00030B/1105
* 9 7 8 8 1 9 8 4 3 1 6 2 2 *